Also by Cameron M. Bracey

Don't Give Up Just Yet, You Still Have A Purpose

Dive Into Your Destiny

Jump Into Faith

Copyright © 2020 by Cameron Bracey

ISBN: 9781733734523

All rights reserved. No part of this publication may be reproduced, distributed, or transmitted in any form or by any means, including photocopying, recording, or other electronic or mechanical methods, without the prior written permission of the publisher, except in the case of brief quotations embodied in critical reviews and certain other noncommercial uses permitted by copyright law.

Introduction

Are you tired of being trapped in your mind? Do you feel like you have a hard time forgiving someone who may have offended you? Do you believe God has more for your life? At some point in time, maybe even today, all of us have felt like we were trapped because of discouragement, unforgiveness, anger, or a lack of faith. Deep down inside, you know that God has prepared a place for you, but your current situation makes it seem as if you'll never get there. Maybe you wanted to be married by 25, but life took you down another road and now you are 30 with no husband, wife, or kids. Maybe you wanted to start your own business by the time you were 30, but there wasn't a bank in sight that would loan the money you needed to bring those ideas to life. If you feel like there is no way out of your current situation, *I'm Breaking Out* is just for you! *I'm Breaking Out* will reveal why you must keep the faith as the wind gets stronger and the waves become heavier. This 100-day devotional will reveal the importance of forgiveness, love, embracing your giants, and walking out on faith even when it seems as if everything and everyone is against you. Over the next 100-days, you will find the courage to break out of poverty, debt, sickness, and your mind! If you feel like you're trapped, it is time for you to break out because God has more for you!

Day 1

New Territory

Think about where you were and who you were in 2010. Some of us were transitioning from middle school to high school while others were transitioning from college to corporate America. You may have been entering a new school where the hallways were filled with hundreds of students who were either focused on how to get to their next class or thinking about what they're going to do after graduation. Maybe you were walking into an organization where the environment was filled with a myriad of individuals that included lawyers, executives, and accountants all of whom were on a mission to get to their next destination. No matter where you were in transition, you had to adjust to the pace and space of your new territory. When God wants to give us new territory, He requires us to leave behind what we were once familiar with. He doesn't give us new territory just to have the same experience as we did in the old. He gives us new territory so that we can accomplish greater things while also being a blessing to others. Don't be afraid to conquer new territory. Don't be intimidated by the vast amount of land you see. When God gives you land, get ready to expand!

Scripture

The Lord had said to Abram, "Leave your native country, your relatives, and your father's family, and go to the land that I will show you. I will make you into a great nation. I will bless you and make you famous, and you will be a blessing to others.

Genesis 12:1-2 NLT

Prayer

God, expand my territory. There is no room for me to grow where I stand, but I know there is much growth that can take place in new land. Allow me to bless others just as You have blessed me. In Jesus name, amen.

Day 2

Financial wealth follows mental wealth

In order to be wealthy in life, you must be wealthy in your mind. What you think is what you'll see. You can't think poor and be rich. You can't think negatively and speak positively. You can't think weak and be strong. You can't think small and expect large. You can't think like a fool and be wise. Your mind must be full of wealth. Many of us check the balances of our bank accounts every day, some may even check every hour, but if you don't check the balance of your mind, you won't see balance in your life. Being wealthy in the mind requires you to think positively when everyone else around you is negative. An individual with mental wealth knows that they are a winner while others may see them as a loser. People with wealthy minds stand tall in faith while others lay down in defeat. Those with a wealthy mind know that what is before them is greater than what is behind them! The thought of failure doesn't stop them from reaching for success. The thought of falling doesn't stop them from climbing. A wealthy mind will take you much further than any amount of money. You can be rich financially and poor mentally. This is why we have so many celebrities and other individuals with a wealth of money who become depressed and have suicidal thoughts because they are poor in the mind. While everyone is telling them how great of a singer, an actor, or an entrepreneur they are, they think less of themselves. A wealthy mind will keep you alive! A wealthy mind will allow you to produce wealth in your life! You will experience wealth not only in your bank account, but in your mind!

Scripture

I am leaving you with a gift—peace of mind and heart. And the peace I give is a gift the world cannot give.

John 14:27 NLT

Prayer

Lord, if there is any place in my mind that is poor, make it rich. Any thoughts that may bring death instead of life, remove them. Depressing thoughts shall not dwell in my mind. I will not allow suicidal thoughts to enter my mind. I give my mind to you, Lord! My mind is healthy! My mind is wealthy! My mind is alive, and not dead! In Jesus name, amen!

Day 3

Love the haters

You don't have time to always worry about the haters. There are going to be people who hate you and everything associated with you whether you're dead or alive. Don't waste a second of your life hating the people that hate you. Don't respond to their negative words with more negative words. Don't live to avenge yourself. Respond with love. Respond by doing what God has called you to do while your haters are wasting time hating on you. God didn't create you to accomplish nothing. He didn't create you to spend your life worrying about what others may have to say about you. He created you to fulfill the purpose He has for you. While the haters are hating on you, love on them. When people choose to curse you, respond by praying for them. When people choose to bring you down, respond by lifting them up. It's easier to hate those who hate you which is why Jesus commanded you and I to love our enemies. He knew there would always be haters, but He also knew that we can only be effective if we love those who hate us. Be bold by expressing love for those who love it when you're crawling, but hate it when you're flying.

Scripture

But I say, love your enemies! Pray for those who persecute you!

Matthew 5:44 NLT

Prayer

Anyone who may be mad at me, Jesus help them find a place in their heart to forgive me. Any negative words that may be thrown at me shall not affect me. I will not become offended because of what people may say or think about me. I will continue to live my life for you, Lord. In Jesus name, amen.

Day 4

Immanuel

You were with Abraham as he left his family to live in a land You prepared for him. You were with Moses as he brought Your people out of Egypt. You're the same God who took Joseph from a well to a cell to a palace. You're the same God who walked with Joshua and his army. You're the same God who introduced Boaz to Ruth. You're the same God who delivered Jonah out of the whale. You're the same God who was in the fire with Shadrach, Meshach, and Abednego. You're the same God who was with Jesus as He gave His life for our sins. You're the same God who closed Paul's eyes to shift his vision. You are always with us! In the middle of the storm or in the midst of a fire, You are with us! There is no reason for us to be afraid because You are Immanuel! It's hard for some people to believe God is with them when they don't have enough money to pay their bills. It can be difficult to know that God is with you when a drunk driver runs a stop sign and hits your child. It's difficult to comprehend how God is with us when it seems as if all Hell has broken loose in our lives. How do you know He's with you? When you're going through things that just don't seem to make sense. When your life gets cloudy and you can't seem to see past the storm, know that God is with you. The Bible tells us that

Moses disappeared into the cloud as he climbed Mt. Sinai to speak to God. When the rain is pouring down on you and you just can't seem to find a moment to dry yourself off, try speaking to God. When the clouds get dark and you don't know what to do, seek God. He is always with you.

Scripture

Look! The virgin will conceive a child! She will give birth to a son, and they will call him Immanuel, which means 'God is with us.'

Matthew 1:23 NLT

Prayer

Whether I am in the pit of a valley or on the peak of a mountaintop, I know that You are with me. In the midst of a storm I know that You are there. When I was lost, You found me. When the enemy tried to kill me You were there to protect me. You are Immanuel! You have and always will be with me! In Jesus name, amen.

Day 5

He knows you by name

Jesus walked around with no jewelry, no Nike's, no special cologne, no Levi's, nothing flashy. He didn't identify Himself with the clothes He wore. He didn't seek gold to prove that He was worthy. He didn't need a degree to prove He was wise. Jesus knew who He was and what He was capable of doing. He didn't need Burberry, Coach, Versace, or a mansion to prove His worth. His confidence, humility, and love spoke louder than any materialistic thing we can ever buy. He didn't need anything flashy because He knew the light inside of Him was brighter than any piece of jewelry. Who are you without the Mercedes, without the mansion, without the degrees, without the shoes, without the jewelry, without the money, and without the clothes? God didn't identify Abraham by the clothes he was wearing. He didn't identify Moses by the jewelry he owned. When we kneel at His feet, none of that will matter. When God calls you, He'll call you by name.

Scripture

"That is why I tell you not to worry about everyday life—whether you have enough food and drink, or enough clothes to wear. Isn't life more than food, and your body more than clothing?"

Matthew 6:25 NLT

Prayer

Before my father and mother were expecting me, You knew my name. As a sinner, You never called me by the name of the sin I committed. You called me by the name You gave me when You breathed life into me. Even when nobody else knows who I am, God, you know me. I am blessed because you know my name. In Jesus name, amen.

Day 6

It's a blessing when it's difficult

While Jesus was on the cross suffocating with nails in His hands and feet and a crown of thorns piercing his head, He prayed for those who were mocking Him. He prayed for the romans who tore the beard off his face and tore the flesh off His back. Before He said, "It is finished," He forgave every single person who may have done Him wrong. He forgave the soldiers who were making bets on His garments as He was on the cross dying. He didn't just forgive these individuals by merely saying, "I forgive you." He took forgiveness to another level by paying the ultimate price. He died for our sins, our transgressions, and our iniquities. He could've easily said, "I forgive you, but I don't love you enough to die for you." It is important that our actions reflect our forgiveness. This doesn't mean you have to die for someone else's wrongdoings, but it's not enough to tell God you forgive someone and then curse them behind their back. You must love those who may have offended you, just as Jesus loves us. Find a place in your heart to pray for those who mock you and laugh at you as God develops you. Find the strength to lift up those who may have kicked you when you were down. Find the passion to care for your loved ones in their old age even though they didn't care for you when you were younger. If you wish to be like Jesus, you must pray when it's difficult to breathe. You must love when it's difficult to forgive. You must have hope when it's difficult to see past the storm.

Scripture

Jesus said, "Father, forgive them, for they don't know what they are doing." And the soldiers gambled for his clothes by throwing dice.

Luke 23:34 NLT

Prayer

Heavenly Father, give me the strength to stand when my legs feel weak. Give me the strength to walk when I can't see where I am going. I will not let fear stop me. I will not let the enemy defeat me. Today may be difficult, but I know that You are shaping me for tomorrow. I know that there is a great blessing on the other side of the storm. Give me the strength to keep pressing! In Jesus name, amen.

Day 7

Win

We all have the desire to win at something in life. For some, that means winning in relationships. For others, that may mean winning on the job. You may want to win the election at your school to become class president while someone else wants to win $50,000 dollars on a scratch off ticket. It doesn't matter what it may be, we all want to win. Unfortunately, many people are losing. Why? Because they have yet to start. They are afraid of starting because they may not have the education or the experience. They are afraid of starting because they don't have the money, or they force themselves to believe that they simply don't have the time. Another reason people lose is because they won't own their mistakes. They won't take ownership of the mountains in front of them or what God has given them. When we think about champions such as Michael Jordan, Kobe Bryant, Tom Brady, or Peyton Manning, they all have something in common; they started NOW and they OWNED the moments. They didn't let their circumstances delay their flights to success. They didn't quit after losing a game. They were determined to win at what they do best. If you want to win in the areas God has gifted you, start now and own every moment. No matter where you are, how much money you have, or what your level of education is, start NOW! OWN every moment. The good, the bad, and the ugly. Then you would have WON! You are a winner! You are destined to win!

Scripture

Jesus was sleeping at the back of the boat with his head on a cushion. The disciples woke him up, shouting, "Teacher, don't you care that we're going to drown?"

Mark 4:38 NLT

Prayer

You don't respond to the thunder crashing or to the waves roaring. You respond to my voice. If I want Your attention, I must call on Your name. When in doubt, I will call on you. When I am afraid, I will call on You. When I am stuck, I will call on You because You are always listening for my voice. In Jesus name, amen.

Day 8

Submission

So many people submit their genitals to someone who wants them for a moment, but they won't submit their heart to the One who will love them for an eternity. Many people don't even realize that they've prostituted themselves to alcohol, drugs, social media, sex, and pornography. They tell God, "I submit myself to You, Lord," but instead of thanking Him first thing in the morning, they check to see how many followers they have on Instagram. They are more worried about snap streaks than a daily prayer streak. You may be reading this thinking to yourself, "I would read my bible daily, but between getting the kids ready for school, getting them on the bus, going to work, making sure someone is at the house before they get home from school, getting home from work, cooking dinner, helping the kids with their homework, giving them a bath, and putting them to bed, I simply don't have the time." Everything you probably thought I'm sure is true, but how many times did you check Snapchat today? How much time did you spend looking up deals on Fashion Nova? How many times did you go on Bleacher report to check the score of the basketball, football, or baseball game? Submission to God means you accept His will for your life. His plan for you will satisfy you more than any man, woman, degree, or job. When you submit yourself to God, you make time for Him every day. If that means you have to wake up a little earlier or go to bed a little later, do what you must because when you make time for God, He will make space for you. Stop checking in with Facebook and start checking in with God.

Scripture

Submit to God, and you will have peace; then things will go well for you.

Job 22:21 NLT

Prayer

Today, I want to submit myself to You, Lord. I submit my thoughts to You. I submit my plan to You. I will submit my attitudes to You. I will submit my heart to you. Anything that I have held onto, God, I submit to you. I am Yours. In Jesus name, amen.

Day 9

Don't lose sight of your vision.

It can be discouraging when your reality doesn't align with your vision. It's tough when your environment doesn't match your destination. As you may know, Joseph had many dreams. He first dreamed of his bundles of grain standing up while his brothers' grains bowed before his. Later, he dreamed of the sun, moon, and stars bowing before him. Joseph's brothers didn't believe in his dreams and thought he was speaking nonsense. The Bible then tells us that his brothers threw him into a well and later sold him into slavery. Joseph went from dreaming about the sun, the moon, and the stars bowing before him to being sold into slavery. I can only imagine what Joseph was thinking and how he felt. I'm sure he was hurt by the betrayal of his brothers and confused because his vision didn't match his reality. Joseph never thought he would end up in a well and then be sold into slavery. I'm pretty sure Joseph thought that someday he would be working in the field with his brothers and everything would go just as he imagined. You and I can relate to that. We can relate to the feeling of discouragement after we dream one thing, but experience another. We envision where we want to go and how we're going to get there, but our map doesn't match God's map. In Joseph's case, his dreams didn't come to fruition until after he had been thrown in a well, sold into slavery, given a job that he was committed to, but didn't love, then thrown into jail because he refused to have sex with a married woman. You may not have the same experiences as Joseph, but you will go through many trials and tribulations before you reach your destination. Don't lose sight of the dream God has given you. He may hide you for a season just like He hid Joseph. It doesn't mean God isn't with you or has forgotten you. It means He is developing you. You're precious in God's eyes and He wants you to experience your dreams to the fullest.

Scripture

Since Joseph was governor of all Egypt and in charge of selling grain to all the people, it was to him that his brothers came. When they arrived, they bowed before him with their faces to the ground.

Genesis 42:6 NLT

Prayer

Heavenly Father, in the areas where I have become blind, give me sight. Open my eyes to things that are of You, Lord. Give me a new perspective. In Jesus name, amen.

Day 10

Loved, not mistaken

You may be reading this today thinking that you're no longer loved because of your past. You may be thinking God wants nothing to do with you because you didn't want anything to do with Him for the past 10, 15, or 20 years. You may have slipped into the trap of pornography or slept with someone who isn't your wife or husband. You probably went to the club last night and got wasted with all your friends knowing that you have to be at church early the next morning. You probably cursed out someone who disrespected you and your family and now you feel as if God can never forgive you for the words that came out of your mouth. Maybe you just lashed out at your mother after she told you the man that raised you isn't your biological father. I want to remind you today, that although you've made mistakes, you're not a mistake. You are loved! Although you've turned your back on God for a season, He hasn't turned His back on you. His arms are always wide open for His children to run into. We all go through a season where we enjoy sin. For some, it may be six months whereas for others it may be seven years. No matter how long that season is, I want you to know that you are loved and not mistaken. God knew what your weaknesses would be when He created you. He knew the family you would be born into before you were in your mother's womb. He knew you would struggle with alcohol and pornography, but that didn't stop Him from loving you. If you're reading this today, always remember that you are loved and not mistaken.

Scripture

For God so loved the world, that he gave his only begotten Son, that whosoever believeth in him should not perish, but have everlasting life.

John 3:16 KJV

Prayer

When I made mistakes, You loved me. When I broke promises, You loved me. When I denied You, You loved me. When I didn't do what You had asked me to do, You still loved me. When others see me my mistakes, You see me. While others may find every reason to hate me, You have every reason to love me. Thank You for loving me even when I didn't deserve to be loved. I love you, Jesus! Amen!

Day 11

Answer the call

If God called you from a house phone, would you answer? If He texted you from an android and the message appeared green on your iPhone, would you respond? If He spoke to you through a burning bush and asked you to remove the socks and shoes from your feet, would you listen? God speaks to us in ways that we would never imagine. If you're a man reading this right now, understand that God will speak to you through your wife. Don't think because she's a woman, God won't communicate to you through her. If you're a woman reading this right now, God will use your husband in ways that may seem odd to you at first just to get your attention. If you're a parent reading this right now, God will take your child or children through different experiences not to only teach them a lesson, but to bring you closer to Him. God may call you to go somewhere outside of your comfort zone to expand your horizons. He may call you to do things that society may not find acceptable because He wants you to be accomplished, not accepted. When God calls you, don't expect Him to be loud. On the other hand, Satan will scream as He tries to talk over God's. Satan will scream you're a loser, but God will whisper you're a winner. Satan will scream you're lost, but God will whisper that you're found. Satan will scream that you're sick, but

God will whisper that you're healed. Listen for God's voice. Answer His call. His voice won't mislead you nor will it ridicule you. Answer God's call.

Scripture

When the Lord saw Moses coming to take a closer look, God called to him from the middle of the bush, "Moses! Moses!" "Here I am!" Moses replied.

Exodus 3:4 NLT

Prayer

Whenever You call me, I will answer. Wherever and whenever you want me to go, I will go. I will be obedient to Your calling for my life. My ears will always be listening for Your voice. It doesn't matter how loud the world may be, all I want to hear is You. I have tuned out the devil and I am now tuned into You, Lord. In Jesus name, amen.

Day 12

God can't be maxed out

The credit card company may say you have a $2,000 limit, but God is limitless. You may be able to max out your credit card, but you can never max out God. He will do things in your life that no man can do. He will move mountains that seem impossible to move. What you've been praying for over 10 years, God will give to you in one day. When the stock market crashes, God is sitting on His throne. When the bank won't loan you any money, God will make your funds sufficient. When your credit score is so low that you can't even purchase a Honda, God sits so high that He'll bless you with a Mercedes. When there was no rain or dew for a few years and there weren't many crops growing for the people to eat, God sent ravens to bring the prophet Elijah bread to eat. When the ravens stopped bringing food, God instructed Elijah to go to Zarephath where there was a woman who would feed him. When Elijah arrived, he asked the woman to bring him a small cup of water and some bread. The woman explained to Elijah that she had no food left in her home. All she had was the few sticks she had gathered, a handful of flour, and a little cooking oil. The woman thought that was the last meal she and her son were going to eat before they die, but Elijah instructed her to not be afraid! Elijah knew what this woman had left was very little, but He also knew God had so much more to give. Elijah instructed the woman to make him some bread first, then to use what's left to cook a meal for the woman and her son. I'm sure that the woman thought Elijah was crazy at first. She probably thought, "Did you not just hear what I told you? I only have a little left for my son and I before we die." But somewhere deep down, this woman had faith to do just what Elijah had instructed her to do. As a result, God made sure that there was always flour and oil left in her containers. When you are down to your last penny, your last slice of bread, your last drop of oil, God will supply you with all of your needs because He cannot be maxed out!

Scripture

And this same God who takes care of me will supply all your needs from his glorious riches, which have been given to us in Christ Jesus.

Philippians 4:19 NLT

Prayer

It doesn't matter how much I call on You, I know You can never be maxed out. Whether I am broke or rich, I know that You will supply all my needs! In Jesus name, amen.

Day 13

You choose what you wear

You may go through hell, but God doesn't want you living there. The devil will try to throw all of his dirty clothes on you to get you there. He wants you to wear a shirt that says anger. On the back of this shirt are the names of your friends who have betrayed you and the family members who may have left you. He wants you to wear a shirt that says depressed. On the back of this shirt will be the date your job laid you off and the dreams you've had that have yet to come to fruition. He wants you to wear a shirt that says stressed. On the back of this shirt will be all the bills that need to be paid and the balance of the funds available in your account which doesn't seem to be enough. The devil's clothes are baggy and will bring you down. They're wrinkly and have a scent that others won't find too pleasing. When you wear the devil's garments, you'll find it harder to forgive others, to love others, and to give unto others. You and I are blessed because we don't have to wear those clothes. We can wear clothes that represent life and not death. We are clothed with forgiveness, love, hope, peace, kindness, and a sound mind. God's clothes allow you and I to love others regardless of their past. His clothes allow us to forgive those who may have offended us. His clothes give us hope in the midst of a storm when it seems all has been lost.

If you want to live in hell after going through it, wear the devil's garments. If you want to live a prosperous life here on Earth and then spend an eternity in heaven, put on God's garments. He'll clothe you with strength to get you there. At the end of the day, you choose what you wear.

Scripture

Come close to God, and God will come close to you. Wash your hands, you sinners; purify your hearts, for your loyalty is divided between God and the world.

James 4:8 NLT

Prayer

I will no longer wear the clothes of the weak and defeated because You created me to be strong and victorious. I will not wear a hat that says "depressed" because I will keep pressing! I will wear the full armor of God! In Jesus name, amen!

Day 14

Stand

Many people today believe they're running towards their destiny, but they have yet to stand in their reality. You may know someone who wants to run wall street, but they won't even stand up for what they believe in on their street. How can you run after your calling if you have yet to stand? God has asked you to stand, yet you remain seated. Jesus didn't pick up the paralyzed man. He told the man to stand! You may be reading this today and feel like you can't relate to the paralyzed man, but maybe you've been paralyzed emotionally. Since your spouse walked out on you, you haven't found the strength to stand in the place where you hurt. You were probably paralyzed mentally after your parents told you for years that you would never be who you aspired to become. Instead of standing in a place where you love what you do, you became paralyzed in a place where the benefits don't benefit you. Jesus knew that for the man to walk, he had to stand. I'm sure all throughout this man's life, people walked by him and paid him no attention. He was known as the paralyzed man who may never stand, until one day they saw him standing right next to Jesus. If you're sitting on the couch waiting for God to carry you to the place He has prepared for you, you'll be sitting there forever. Before you can walk towards your destiny you, must stand in your reality. Before you can run in your destiny, you must walk through the journey. All you have to do is stand!

Scripture

So I will prove to you that the Son of Man has the authority on earth to forgive sins." Then Jesus turned to the paralyzed man and said, "Stand up, pick up your mat, and go home!"

Matthew 9:6 NLT

Prayer

If I want to get to the place You have prepared for me, I must stand. I will no longer lay in the doubts of my enemies, but I will stand in the place of Your faith. I may be knocked down, but I won't be knocked out. I will stand in the midst of every trial! In Jesus name, amen.

Day 15

Accomplished not Accepted

If you died today, what impact would you have left behind? If an angel told you that your last day on Earth was today, what would you strive to accomplish? Would you publish those books that you've had saved on your laptop for the past 20 years? Would you write the songs that God placed on your heart 10 years ago? Would you write that play about your life that you once thought could never come to life? I know you're reading this right now thinking about what you would do or where you would travel. Today is the day where you strive to become who you were born to be. Ask yourself, are you proud of who you've become? If the answer to that question is no, then you need to re-evaluate what you're doing with your time. Maybe you need to spend more time with your family. Maybe you need to do what you've been called to do instead of what others told you to do. If you want to be accomplished, you must be okay with not being accepted. You may have to sacrifice some relationships and weekends with your friends, but what makes you unique is that you would rather be accomplished than accepted. You made an impact when you entered the world, now make an impact before you leave. You were born to be great! You were born to be prosperous! You were born to be successful!

Scripture

It is the same with my word. I send it out, and it always produces fruit. It will accomplish all I want it to, and it will prosper everywhere I send it.

Isaiah 55:11 NLT

Prayer

You were never focused on being accepted. You never let the opinions of others stop you from fulling Your purpose. Jesus, I will no longer focus on being accepted. I will no longer focus on fitting in with the crowd. Let Your will be done in my life. In Jesus name, amen.

Day 16

Address your giant

Before you can overcome a challenge, you must address the giant. When the Israelites saw Goliath, they became intimidated and fearful. The Bible tells us that Goliath was nine feet tall and wore a bronze coat of mail that weighed 125 pounds. Goliath challenged the Israelites to send out one of their warriors to fight him. The deal was if the Israelite defeated Goliath, the Philistines would be Israel's slaves, but if Goliath defeated the Israelite, the Israelites would become the Philistine's slaves. Fear then struck Saul and his army because they didn't know how to address Goliath. As a result, for forty days, Goliath stood in front of Israel's army waiting for a brave warrior to accept his challenge. How long has a giant stood in front of you because you won't address it? How long has alcohol consumed you? How long has stress been holding you captive? How long has fear kept you from addressing the giants that stand tall in your life? Maybe you've been intimidated by a giant for over 40 years. Maybe you feel like you don't have the weapons or the strength to bring it down. Maybe you lack faith in God who has given you the tools, the wisdom, and the strength to address your giant. In order to overcome an addiction, a weakness, or a challenge, you must address the problem. Don't waste time or lose sight of your where you're going because of a giant that is standing in front of you. Address the giant, then you'll overcome the challenge.

Scripture

"Don't worry about this Philistine," David told Saul. "I'll go fight him!"

1 Samuel 17:32 NLT

Prayer

I don't care how tall my giant may stand! I don't care how strong it may appear! God, you have made me victorious! I will approach my giant in faith, not in fear! I won't put on man's armor because I am already wearing Your armor. I'm not worried about my giant today or the giant I may face tomorrow because I know You will give me the strength to defeat all of my enemies! In Jesus name, amen.

Day 17

Assess Your Attitude

Once you've addressed your giant, you must assess your attitude. David, who was a shepherd's boy, didn't appear to be intimidated or frightened by Goliath's size. David was focused on taking down Goliath. While the Israelite army was paralyzed by fear, David went on to tell King Saul that he's up for the challenge. Saul didn't believe that David would be able to take down Goliath because David was only a boy. Despite Saul's doubts, David was persistent. He reminded Saul that as a shepherd's boy, it was his duty to protect his father's sheep. David had to fight both a lion and a bear. Goliath was no different than any giant he had previously faced. After being reminded of what his responsibilities entailed as a shepherd's boy, Saul decided to let David go up against Goliath. When you are about to face your giant, don't let others talk you out of what God has equipped you to do. When the doctor says it will be impossible for you to ever run again, remind him that the giant ahead of you is no different than the giants behind you. When your boss laughs after you've told them that you will someday own the company, remind them that the season you're in now is preparing you for everything God has promised you. Don't become defeated by someone's lack of faith. Don't become discouraged when your friends don't see the fortitude of your heart. After you've addressed the giant, assess your attitude.

Scripture

The Lord who rescued me from the claws of the lion and the bear will rescue me from this Philistine!" Saul finally consented. "All right, go ahead," he said. "And may the Lord be with you!"

1 Samuel 17:37 NLT

Prayer

Lord, I ask that You give me the strength to assess my attitudes in the midst of every trial. I ask that You strengthen my heart to forgive others when it's easier to be angry. I ask that You give me the strength to keep on pressing even when I feel like quitting. You are my strength. In Jesus name, amen.

Day 18

Express Your Faith

After King Saul decided to allow David to accept Goliath's challenge, he tried giving him his armor and a sword. Although the gear was meant to protect David, he explained to Saul that he wasn't used to wearing that much armor. Instead of the armor and the king's sword, all David needed was a slingshot and five smooth stones. When Goliath saw David, he saw a boy who probably weighed no more than 130 lbs. with no armor, and a slingshot with five stones as his weapons. Although David appeared to be a lightweight, the God he served was and still is the heaviest of heavyweights! Goliath thought David was no match for him, but really Goliath was no match for David. David's strength was his faith in God. Goliath's weakness was the faith he had in himself. As David and Goliath approached one another, David expressed the faith he had in God. He knew God would deliver Goliath and all the Philistines over to Israel. Sure enough, what he spoke came to pass. When you are facing a giant, do you tell it what God can and will do or do you explain to it what you're able to do? When we approach our giants, we must express that the battle is already won. We must not express fear or doubt. By doing such a thing, you're giving your giant more power than it really has. Don't let the appearance of your situation deter you away from your destination. The bigger a giant is, the harder it falls!

Scripture

Today the Lord will conquer you, and I will kill you and cut off your head. And then I will give the dead bodies of your men to the birds and wild animals, and the whole world will know that there is a God in Israel!

1 Samuel 17:46 NLT

Prayer

If I am at church, I will express my faith. If I am at home, I will express my faith. If I am at school, I will express my faith. If I am at work, I will express my faith. If I am overseas, I will express my faith. If I am in the midst of a battle, I will express my faith. It doesn't matter where I am or what giant stands in front of me, I will express my faith in You, Lord. In Jesus name, amen.

Day 19

Preparation

Many people declare the arrival of their blessing before preparing for it. If you want to thrive in what God is about to give you, whether it be a new job, a promotion, or the resources to start your own business, you must prepare for it. How does one do so? You prepare by praying, fasting, and resting. James tells us that the earnest prayer of a righteous person has great power and produces wonderful results. Prayer strengthens you for the battle that lies ahead of you. Jesus prayed in the garden of Gethsemane seeking His father for strength before He was betrayed and arrested. Fasting gives you the strength to resist temptations. When you receive your blessing, God wants you to be disciplined. He wants you to be able to say no to the things that may be pleasing to the eye, but are lethal to our body and soul. Jesus had been fasting for forty days and nights when Satan tempted Him in the desert. Although Jesus was physically weak, He was spiritually strong. At one point, Satan offered Jesus all the kingdoms in the world, but Jesus knew His kingdom was not of this world. Before you receive your blessing, you must also rest. God won't deliver the blessing to you if you're not fully restored. God wants you to be able to enjoy the reward He is about to give you, but you can't do that if you worked so hard that you never gave your body a chance to heal and your mind time to rest. In order to be ready for the blessing when it arrives, you must prepare for it now.

Scripture

The earnest prayer of a righteous person has great power and produces wonderful results.

James 5:16 NLT

Prayer

God, give me patience in this season of preparation. I know that You are taking me through the fire to strengthen me, not to harm me. I know that You are carving me for the place you have prepared for me. Your training camp is like no other, which is why I will come out stronger. I am planted in You, Lord. In Jesus name, amen.

Day 20
I Am

After God spoke to Moses through a burning bush, Moses had already anticipated telling the Israelites that the God of Heaven's Armies spoke to him. Moses knew the people would respond by asking what God's name is. When Moses asked God how he should respond when the people ask him this, God replied, "I Am Who I Am." When you say, "I Am," what you're really saying is, "God is." Instead of saying, "I am weak," you should say, "I Am strong," because our God is strong. God doesn't respond to "I am sick. I am a loser. I am broke. I am a nobody." God isn't any of those things and neither are we. What you must realize is that God expresses Himself through you. When you call on Him, you are to speak life and not death. You should be saying things like, "I Am blessed! I Am healed! I Am whole! I Am a winner! I Am wealthy! I Am somebody!" Those two words can either be your call out to God or they can just be another waste of words. You are loved. You are whole. You are forgiven. You are worthy. You are accomplished. Be mindful when you say, "I Am."

Scripture

God replied to Moses, "I Am Who I Am. Say this to the people of Israel: I Am has sent me to you."

Exodus 3:14 NLT

Prayer

I am loved. I am whole. I am forgiven. I am not forgotten. I am victorious. I am healthy. I am blessed. I am joyful. I am cheerful. I am strong. I am wise. I am worthy. I am accomplished. I am a winner. I am wealthy. I am Yours! In Jesus name, amen.

Day 21

Two is better than one

When God said, "It is not good for man to be alone," He didn't give Adam a luxurious car, a mansion, a phone, or a million dollars. He blessed Adam with a woman by the name of Eve! He could've given Adam any of those things that many men THINK will make them happy, but God knew that Eve was far more valuable than any materialistic object. She was Adam's Ferrari, his mansion, his iPhone 11, his $100 million dollar contract! God gave Adam all those things in a woman! To every husband who may be reading this today, value your wife. To every wife reading this, value your husband. God brought you two together to become one. You can accomplish much more together than you can apart. When you and your spouse support each other's dreams, you will enjoy the rewards with one another. When you function as one, you will conquer more territory. The Bible tells us that any man who finds a wife finds a good thing, and finds favor with the Lord. Your wife adds not only flavor to your life, but favor!

Scripture

Then the Lord God said, "It is not good for the man to be alone. I will make a helper who is just right for him."

Genesis 2:18 NLT

Prayer

I cannot endure this life alone. God, I need You. The partner You've blessed me with, God I thank You. You knew that Two is better than one. You knew that my husband and I or my wife and I can accomplish more together than we could apart. You are the center of our relationship and You are the center of our lives. In Jesus name, amen.

Day 22

The gates shall fall

When the enemy closes a gate, he is trying to prevent God's warriors from overthrowing what he temporarily has control over. Jericho's gates were shut because the people were afraid of the Israelites. Although the gates were closed, God had already given the land over to Joshua and his army. In today's society, these closed gates are ones where God's people can have the biggest impact. The enemy doesn't want God's people to come into the entertainment industry. He knows that if we get our foot in the door, the gospel will reach billions of people all around the world. If we get our foot in the door of government, policies will be made to honor God and not man. If we get our foot in the door of education, prayer will make its way back into our schools. If we get our foot in the door of healthcare, there will be more healing taking place in the hospitals because we will have more men and women employed who rely on God more than the medication. God commanded Joshua and his army to march around the walls of Jericho once a day and seven times on the seventh day. After they marched around the walls of Jericho for the seventh time on the seventh day, the walls of Jericho collapsed, and God's people were given the land. Now we may not march around a hospital, the white house, or our schools every day, but we can pray for them. We can pray so much that God will swing open the gates of our government, our schools, our hospitals, and the entertainment industry for us to go in and spread His word. The gates shall fall for you and I to stand tall.

Scripture

When the people heard the sound of the rams' horns, they shouted as loud as they could. Suddenly, the walls of Jericho collapsed, and the Israelites charged straight into the town and captured it.

Joshua 6:20 NLT

Prayer

I will keep on marching until every gate in my life has fallen. I may not see a pebble fall or a door open, but I know that as long as I keep on marching, You will bring down every gate in my life. Any wall, any barrier, or any gate that stands tall in my life will fall today! In Jesus name, amen.

Day 23

Invest in Heaven

Millions of people all around the world love to make investments. Whether they invest in the stock market, rental property, or land, investing, like anything else, has its pros and cons. While making an investment can earn you a lot of money, you also take the chance of losing more than you earn. If you've invested in the stock market and the economy crashes, you can lose thousands, maybe even millions of dollars over a short period of time. Maybe you know someone who has invested their money into rental properties. While this can also be an opportunity for one to make more money, these individuals may have to spend hundreds of thousands of dollars on maintenance expenses along with the risk of losing money if their tenants don't pay the rent on time. Another investment opportunity that many people seek is owning land. It may seem at first that one can't lose money owning land, but that is far from the truth. Owning land also carries its risks such as stock market crashes and natural disasters that may have a negative impact on the land you own. Although investments carry many risks, investing in heaven has no risks. Jesus tells us that it is wise to store our treasures in heaven where moths and rust can't destroy, and thieves cannot break in and steal. When you give your tithes and offerings to God, you aren't only investing in Earthly rewards, but your heavenly reward also. While you may not be able to watch heaven's market like the stock market, you don't ever have to worry about heaven's market losing value. When you invest in God, He will invest in you. The rewards of heaven are more promising than any other reward. Before you invest in anything else, invest in heaven.

Scripture

Store your treasures in heaven, where moths and rust cannot destroy, and thieves do not break in and steal.

Matthew 6:20 NLT

Prayer

God, I will invest my time in You. I will invest my money into Your kingdom. I will invest my mind in You. You invested in me when You created me. I want to return that investment to You, Lord. I give myself to You. There is no greater investment than investing in You, Jesus. My harvest will be much greater when I invest in You instead of a stock. In Jesus name, amen.

Day 24

Faith Heals

The Bible briefly mentions a woman who had suffered with bleeding for twelve years. Now I want you to think about what this woman had to go through. No doctor was able to help her and probably no man wanted to marry her. This woman was most likely kicked to the curb by society. One day as Jesus was walking by, she decided to walk up behind Him to touch the hymn of His garment because she knew she would be healed. When Jesus turned around, He told her to be encouraged because her faith made her well. If you were this woman, would you have the faith to go outside into a crowd where people look down on you because of a disease you cannot control? You may say yes, or you may say no. No matter what your answer may be, remember that this woman's faith is what set her free. Maybe you've been battling cancer for 12 years or maybe debt has held you captive for the past 20 years. Some of your family and friends may recognize you as the woman with the issue of breast cancer or the man with the issue of unemployment. Maybe you or someone you know has been a drug addict or an alcoholic for the past 10 years. You may not be able to physically touch the hymn of His garment like this woman did, but you can have faith like hers. Your faith will heal you! Your faith will deliver you! You are set free!

Scripture

For she thought, "If I can just touch his robe, I will be healed." Jesus turned around, and when he saw her he said, "Daughter, be encouraged! Your faith has made you well." And the woman was healed at that moment.

Matthew 9:21-22 NLT

Prayer

Lord, I want to have the faith that the woman with the issue of blood had. She knew that if she just touched Your robe she would be healed. I know that if I call on You, You will respond. If I ask You for something, You will answer my prayers with something greater than I asked for. My faith is in You, Lord. In Jesus name, amen.

Day 25

The Farm

When you hear someone mention a farm, you immediately think about all the animals such as the cows, pigs, horses, and chickens. You may even think about the crops that are grown in the field such as the corn, wheat, and rice. Although that's what a farm is here on Earth, I am referencing the farm that Jesus talks about in Matthew. He tells us that He is the farmer, the field is the world, we are the seeds He plants, and the weeds are those who worship the devil. You and I are seeds. God didn't plant us to be underground our entire lives. He filled us with rich nutrients to nourish others. He became poor so that His seeds may become rich. Our farmer will forever provide for us. He will give you the right amount of sunlight and rain needed to flourish. He will protect you from the weeds that may try to prevent you from growing into a tree. How you can identify a weed from a seed? Weeds roots don't run deep whereas seeds will grow roots that run deep into the soil. The more you grow, the closer you get to Him. The more you grow, the closer you are to fulfilling the purpose He has for you. No predator nor any weed will destroy you. You are a seed of God. You may appear small at first, but you will grow to be great. The enemy will try to tear you down, but if you allow God to water while your roots are developing, there is no attack from the enemy that will uproot you. What God plants will forever stand.

Scripture

Jesus replied, "The Son of Man is the farmer who plants the good seed. The field is the world, and the good seed represents the people of the Kingdom. The weeds are the people who belong to the evil one."

Matthew 13:37-38 NLT

Prayer

You planted me to do great things here on Earth. The enemy will not pull me away from You because my faith is deeply rooted in You, Lord! You watered me with Your word which gives me life. You are my sunlight which gives me the strength to grow. In Jesus name, amen.

Day 26

Look Up

When Jesus told the disciples to feed the people, the disciples told Jesus that all they had was five loaves of bread and two fish. This is a moment where the disciples had no clue how Jesus was going to feed all the people who were present that day. If you were there, I am sure you would have thought the same. It was within that same moment when Jesus took the basket with the five loaves of bread and two fish and looked up at heaven to bless the food. As Jesus began to break the bread up for the disciples to serve the people, there was enough for all 5,000 men and their families to eat. There was so much food that Matthew tells us there were 12 baskets of leftovers. Although this was one of Jesus' greatest miracles, what many tend to look over in this scripture is that Jesus looked UP. He didn't look down to see what was available because He knew that God would make more than enough available. When food is running low in your home, don't look to the fridge for more food to appear. When money is getting tight, don't check your account hoping that more money will appear. When your marriage isn't the same as it was when you and your spouse first got married, don't look for another man or woman. Look up at God! He is the source! He is the One who will make food available for you and your family. He is the One who will open up doors so that you have multiple streams of income and never have to worry about money getting tight again. He is the One who will light the fire between you and your spouse so that you two don't fall apart. When a team loses a game or a tournament, you usually hear the coach telling their team to keep their heads up. I am telling you to look up. Look up at the source and not down at the resource.

Scripture

Jesus took the five loaves and two fish, looked up toward heaven, and blessed them. Then, breaking the loaves into pieces, he kept giving the bread and fish to the disciples so they could distribute it to the people.

Luke 9:16 NLT

Prayer

When the money is short and the food is low, I will look up to You. When the enemy knocks me down, I will look up to You. When I feel lonely, I will look up to You. I will no longer look down at my problems. I will only look up to You. In Jesus name, amen.

Day 27

If You Doubt, You'll Sink

When the disciples saw Jesus walking on water, they thought He was a ghost until He told them to not be afraid. Hearing His voice wasn't enough for Peter. Peter said, "Lord, if it is really You, tell me to come to you, walking on the water." Jesus told Peter to come. As Peter started walking on water, the Bible tells us that he became terrified after seeing the wind and the waves and began to sink. When Jesus reached out to grab Peter, He told him, "You have so little faith. Why did you doubt me?" See, Peter started to sink because he doubted Jesus in the midst of a storm. Peter thought he wouldn't be able to stand because of the strength of the winds and waves. He forgot that Jesus controls the winds and the waves. He forgot about the time when Jesus told the water to be still. He doubted the power of God. When you doubt God, you'll sink. People sink into depression because they doubt that God has given them strength to keep on pressing. People sink into addiction because they doubt the power of Jesus can set them free. People sink into poverty because they doubt the creativity God has given them to deliver them to their destiny. Marriages sink because many couples doubt that God will bring them through. Businesses sink, both profit and not-for-profit, because when God wants to expand their territory or increase their faith by calling them to step on water where the waves are strong and the wind is heavy, they doubt that God will carry them through. While the doubtful sink, the faithful stand.

Scripture

"You have so little faith," Jesus said. "Why did you doubt me?"

Matthew 14:31 NLT

Prayer

God, forgive me if I have ever doubted you. I apologize that I went left when You told me to go right. When You told me to stay focused on You, I decided to look around because I was afraid that I would miss out on my wife or my husband. The only reason I began to drown is because I doubted the plans You had for my life. I will no longer doubt You. I will only have faith in You and Your promises! In Jesus name, amen.

Day 28

God's Plan

After Jesus told His disciples that He will rise again on the third day after being put to death by the religious leaders, Peter pulled Him to the side and said, "Heaven forbid, Lord, this will never happen to you!" Matthew tells us that Jesus looked at Peter and said, "Get away from me, Satan! You are a dangerous trap to me. You are seeing things merely from a human point of view, not from God's." When you read the text, it's easy to think that Jesus was calling Peter, Satan, but that wasn't the case. When Jesus responded, He wasn't speaking to Peter, He was rebuking Satan. Jesus knew that Satan's plan has and always will be to prevent us from fulfilling God's purpose for our lives. Now, imagine how this made Peter feel since He didn't quite understand what Jesus was saying. Here is the man who Jesus built His church upon. A man who walked with Jesus side by side every day. Peter was probably hurt, maybe even confused because he was only speaking from a place of love and not evil. Like many of us, he didn't want to see any pain inflicted upon his friend and only wanted what he thought was best for Jesus. You may have family or friends who think like Peter. When you tell them that someday you're going to win a Grammy, they may support you, but out of love they want to protect you. They might tell you to seek a 9-5 job with great benefits because it is safe. Others may encourage you to apply to an industrial organization where you can make $70,000-$80,000 a year because the chances of failing are small. Jesus teaches us here that God's plan is and always will be greater than our own. If your plan for your children's lives doesn't align with God's plan, don't encourage them to go the route you believe to be safe. Encourage them to step out on the water with Jesus. God's plan is greater than your own. His plan may be a little scary at first, but you won't ever regret taking that leap of faith. You will reap many rewards for staying on God's path.

Scripture

But Peter took him aside and began to reprimand him for saying such things. "Heaven forbid, Lord," he said. "This will never happen to you!" Jesus turned to Peter and said, "Get away from me, Satan! You are a dangerous trap to me. You are seeing things merely from a human point of view, not from God's."

Matthew 16:22-23 NLT

Prayer

I know Your plan is much greater than anything I could ever imagine. I know Your plan is to prosper and to not harm me. In Jesus name, amen.

Day 29

Pregnant with Greatness

When God plants a seed inside of you, you can either give birth to what He's given you or you can abort His purpose for your life. You may be pregnant with a chain of restaurants, but you are afraid to push because you don't believe anyone will eat the meals you have prepared. You may be pregnant with books, but you abort the ideas that God has given you because you don't think you have what it takes to write a New York Best Seller. Maybe you're pregnant with a play that will bring millions of families together, but since your teachers told you that your writing will never be good enough, you abort the thought of even developing a script. Pregnancy is the opportunity to give birth to a legacy. When Manoah's wife was pregnant with Samson, God told his wife that the child will rescue Israel from the Philistines. Imagine if Manoah's wife would've aborted Samson. She would've been acting out based on her feelings instead of God's plan. As a result, Israel would've continued to be slaves to the Philistine's. Before Mary was pregnant with Jesus, an angel appeared before Mary and told her that Jesus will be the Son of God whose kingdom will never end. If Mary would've aborted Jesus, you and I both would not be living today. The grace and mercy that God has for us wouldn't exist because His son wouldn't have paid the ultimate price. When you're pregnant, think about the legacy you would leave behind with your child or that business. Think about the countless number of doors that can open if you just deliver what God has given you. You are pregnant with greatness!

Scripture

You will become pregnant and give birth to a son, and his hair must never be cut. For he will be dedicated to God as a Nazirite from birth. He will begin to rescue Israel from the Philistines."

Judges 13:5 NLT

Prayer

Lord, I know that I am pregnant with greatness. You have given me life so that I may give life to the gifts You have impregnated me with. Although it may be painful at times, I will keep on pushing. I may begin to feel a little lightheaded, but I will keep on going. Thank you for impregnating me with greatness! In Jesus name, amen.

Day 30

Build Before the Flood

Have you been preparing for your flood? When God says He is going to open up the floodgates of Heaven and pour out a blessing over your life, you must be ready! When God told Noah to build a boat, He gave Noah the wisdom to build an ark. This ark was beyond any man's idea. As Noah was building the ark, people from all over laughed at Him because they didn't understand what He was preparing for. It turned out, the same people who were laughing at Noah are the same people who died in the flood. Don't listen to the people nor give attention to those who doubt what you're building. If you want to publish a book, you must write down the ideas that come to mind because the book won't write itself. If you want to establish a clothing line, you may have to start putting money into your own pieces of fabric and not Versace. You must stay true to what God has instructed you to do. As you're writing that book, building that company, or developing that website, remember that God invested in you when He created you. God will do things in your life that you had never imagined. Build before the flood! Your ark will save you!

Scripture

So God said to Noah, "I have decided to destroy all living creatures, for they have filled the earth with violence. Yes, I will wipe them all out along with the earth! "Build a large boat from cypress wood and waterproof it with tar, inside and out. Then construct decks and stalls throughout its interior.

Genesis 6:13-14 NLT

Prayer

I will continue to build before You pour out a blessing on my life! I don't want to drown in my blessing when it was meant for me to float on! I will build when others don't believe in me. I will build when no one else can see what I'm building for. I will keep on building! In Jesus name, amen.

Day 31

Hosanna

As Jesus entered into Jerusalem on a donkey, the people started shouting, "Hosanna! Hosanna! Hosanna!" What the people were saying was, "Blessings on the one who comes in the name of the Lord! Praise God in the highest heaven!" It's easy to praise God when the crops are flourishing, and business is thriving. "Hosanna! My bills are paid! Hosanna! There is food on the table! Hosanna! I'm not living from paycheck to paycheck! Hosanna! I earned more money this year than I did last year! Hosanna! My spouse and I are about to give birth!" It's great to praise God when life is flowing smoothly, but you must also praise Him in the face of adversity. When the money is short, say Hosanna! When you don't get the promotion you've been hoping for, say Hosanna! When you don't get into the school you've always dreamed of attending, say Hosanna! When your friends throw you in the fire, say Hosanna! When your child goes left after you've told them to go right, say Hosanna! Sing your praises unto God when the fire gets hotter, when the waves get stronger, and when the wind gets heavier! If you praise Him in the valley, you'll praise Him at the mountaintop. If you praise Him on the water, you'll praise Him on land! Praise God! He is the Almighty One!

Scripture

*'Blessed is the kingdom of our father David
That comes in the name of the Lord!
Hosanna in the highest!"'*

Mark 11:10 NKJV

Prayer

When I have no money, I will sing Hosanna. When the doctor gives me a report that I didn't expect, I will sing Hosanna. When my friends betray me, I will sing Hosanna. When I'm in the dark and don't know where else to go, I will sing Hosanna. No matter what situation I may be in, I will sing Hosanna! In Jesus name, amen.

Day 32

Impress God

Many people today are focused on impressing man instead of God. It's impressive when someone buys the latest apple product. It's impressive when you see someone driving down the street in a car that costs as much as your house. It's impressive when your friends are wearing a pair of Jordan's that have yet to be released. It may be impressive to your friends when you own a multi-million-dollar home. It may be impressive to your family when you're able to buy your parents their dream home or their dream cars. It's impressive when you have over a million followers on Instagram. It's impressive when you have 3.5 million subscribers on YouTube. It's impressive when you start a new trend on TikTok that everybody wants to follow. While all of these things may be impressive here on Earth, they're not impressive to God. The number of followers you have on Instagram doesn't impress God. The number of people that are subscribed to your YouTube channel doesn't impress God. The 15-million-dollar home you own with a Ferrari parked in the garage does not impress God. Your skintight Easter dress with the fancy hat doesn't impress God. Your decked-out Easter suit does not impress God. If you want to impress God, worship Him when nobody else will. Praise Him when the world wants to throw you into the fire. Step out on the water when He tells you to. Give God a sacrificial offering. Be faithful while the world is fearful. Instead of Netflix and chill, study your Bible and be still. The things that impress others don't always impress God. If you want to impress God, you must do the opposite of what the world may approve.

Scripture

Carefully determine what pleases the Lord.

Ephesians 5:10 NLT

Prayer

God, I want to impress You and nobody else! Making you smile makes me smile. When I know that I've made you proud, I am filled with so much joy. I want to please you before I please anyone else. In Jesus name, amen.

Day 33

Hidden, Not Forgotten

Maybe you're in a season where you feel like nobody recognizes you for what you're capable of. Have you designed clothes that nobody will take the time to try on because what you've created isn't by Nike, Versace, or Burberry? Have you developed a computer program that will advance technology, but nobody supports it because it doesn't have Apple's label on it? Maybe you've written three or four New York Best-Sellers but haven't received recognition because nobody recognizes the author. It can be discouraging when God has anointed you, but nobody recognizes you. After you've done everything God has asked you to do and nothing happens, you begin to feel as if He has forgotten you. I want to tell you today that God has hidden you. He hasn't forgotten you. He won't forget the books you wrote. He won't forget the clothes you've designed. He won't forget the meals you've prepared. God anointed you, but He had to put you in a cave to protect you. After David was anointed to be the next king of Israel, he later found himself hiding in a cave from King Saul, who was trying to kill him. It's difficult to be anointed and in a cave. You may find it easier to be mad at everyone who doesn't recognize you in the season that God has hidden you. Don't give people credit for God hiding you. Don't blame them for God protecting you. Don't waste your time committing to memory who doesn't support you now. Instead of soaking in all of that negative energy while you're in your cave, take the time to pray. Use your cave to grow closer with God. Use your cave to mature into the person He created you to be. Embrace your cave! You are being hidden and have not been forgotten.

Scripture

But as it happened, David and his men were hiding farther back in that very cave!

1 Samuel 24:3 NLT

Prayer

I may be on a boat during a flood, but I know You haven't forgotten me. I may be in a cave, but I know You are only hiding me. In the seasons I am hidden, I understand that there is a great reason. You are protecting me. You are developing me. You are strengthening me. In Jesus name, amen.

Day 34

God Won't Throw in the Towel

Your boxing match with life may last for 50, 60, 70, 80, 90, or even 100 years. There will be battles in life that will hit you as fast as a lightweight. There will be other battles that'll hit you as hard as a heavyweight. Whether the jab was quick, or the uppercut made you stumble, God won't throw in the towel. Whether your child lies to you or your spouse cheats on you, God won't throw in the towel. It doesn't matter if your car broke down in the middle of the expressway or somebody stole your car while you and your family were on vacation, God won't throw in the towel. Maybe you want God to throw in the towel after Satan delivered a left hook 20 years into the fight. You may want God to throw in the towel after the devil took a blow at your ribs 40 years into the fight. You may want God to throw in the towel after the devil busted your left eye 60 years into the fight. You may want God to throw in the towel after Satan knocked you down 80 years into the fight. When your vision has diminished in your left eye, God won't throw in the towel. When a few of your ribs have been broken making it more and more difficult to breathe, God won't throw in the towel. You are a warrior of God! He didn't create you just for the devil to defeat you! He knows that as long as you have faith in Him, you will be victorious. When the romans tore the flesh off of Jesus' back and hammered nails into His hands and feet, He had the power to call on His angels to stop everything, yet He endured through the pain, the suffering, the bleeding, and the suffocating and through it all, He overcame! You have the strength to overcome! Wipe off your face and stand back up! The devil doesn't know WHOSE he is messing with!

Scripture

"Don't you realize that I could ask my Father for thousands of angels to protect us, and he would send them instantly?"

Matthew 26:53 NLT

Prayer

The enemy may hit me in my eye, but I won't lose my vision. He may hit me in my ribs, but I won't stop breathing. He may knock me down, but he won't knock me out. And through it all, You won't throw in the towel because You have made me victorious. Even when I can't see how I'm going to get out, You have already made a way out. In Jesus name, amen.

Day 35

Again

When the devil labels you as a failure, but God created you to be a winner, you must do it again. After you've been trying to fly time after time, but you keep falling out of the sky, you must stand up and do it again. When a basketball player misses their first free throw attempt, do they not shoot again? When a baseball player strikes out, does he not approach the plate again? When a mother pushes during labor, does she not have to push over and over again? When a student fails a test, are they not given a chance to pass the class again? The key to overcoming failure is by doing it again. The key to winning is repetition. Consistency and persistency will get you to your destiny. When you want to grow larger arms, you must do bicep curls and triceps extension again and again. If you want larger glutes, you must do squats again and again. If you want a larger chest, you must do pushups again and again. When you fall, the devil doesn't want you to get back up. He expects you to sit there crying and complaining that you never achieved what you believed. But if you stand up again, if you pray again, if you push again, the devil will become threatened because he is now aware that God has given you the strength to do it again and again. Do you have what it takes to stand again? Do you have the strength to pray again? Do you have the strength to run again?

Scripture

For a righteous man may fall seven times and rise again, but the wicked shall fall by calamity.

Proverbs 24:16 NKJV

Prayer

I will stand again. I will walk again. I will see again. I will talk again. I will pray again. No matter how many times I may fall, I will keep on standing again and again. In Jesus name, amen.

Day 36

Blessed, Not Stressed

It has been scientifically proven that stress kills. Stress can give you a heart attack. Stress can cause friction between you and your spouse. Stress can decrease your vision. Stress can increase your blood pressure. Stress will cause one to have suicidal thoughts. When we become stressed, it's easy to forget that we're blessed. It's easy to stress when you don't receive the health report you were hoping for, but don't forget you're blessed because we serve a God who heals. You may become stressed when the mortgage company sends you an eviction notice, but you're blessed because God is with you! You become stressed when the world hates you for being different, but you're blessed because God loves you for being His! Whether you're standing on the boat or walking on the water, you're blessed! If you're in the well, you're blessed! If you're in the palace, you're blessed! You can be in a den full of lions, yet you're blessed! The world may want to throw you into the fire, but it'll soon realize that it can't kill you because you're blessed! The devil tried to kill you in that automobile accident last year, but you're blessed! The enemy tried destroying your marriage, but your marriage is blessed! The enemy tried taking you out with a bullet, but as you prayed no weapon formed against me shall prosper, God blessed you! You are blessed!

Scripture

Then Jesus said, "Come to me, all of you who are weary and carry heavy burdens, and I will give you rest. Take my yoke upon you. Let me teach you, because I am humble and gentle at heart, and you will find rest for your souls. For my yoke is easy to bear, and the burden I give you is light."

Matthew 11:28-30 NLT

Prayer

I refuse to become stressed when You have blessed me. When the enemy attacks me with an eviction notice, I will remind him how much You have blessed me. When the enemy wants to attack with a negative doctor's report, I will remind him how blessed I am that I serve a God will turn that report around. I am blessed! In Jesus name, amen.

Day 37

Disconnection

God will try to protect you by disconnecting you from those who are no good for you. Any teenager or young adult reading this today, if the connection between you and your boyfriend or girlfriend gets weak, stop trying to reconnect by having sex. The sex won't reboot the connection God has disconnected. If you two weren't praying together, God sees no reason for you two to stay together. If you're reading this today and the connection between you and your childhood friend has become disconnected, seek God before you try connecting with your friend again. Before God can take you to a new level where the connection is 5G instead of 4G, he must disconnect you from the 3G provider. You may be a businessman or a businesswoman reading this today who has become disconnected with the clients who you thought made it possible for you to take your organization to another level. Your clients may have a played a role in the success of your business, but they aren't your providers. God had to disconnect you from your clients to make you realize that He is the one Who gave you the ability to build your company from the ground up. If you aren't connected to God, He won't connect you with anyone else. God doesn't disconnect us to harm us. He disconnects us to protect us so that He can elevate us. Your disconnection is a precursor to your elevation.

Scripture

'Therefore, come out from among unbelievers, and separate yourselves from them, says the Lord. Don't touch their filthy things, and I will welcome you.

2 Corinthians 6:17 NLT

Prayer

Lord, I want to reconnect with You. I am blessed to say that in order to talk to You, I don't need Wi-Fi or cellular data. All I need is for my heart to be open and willing to receive your Holy Spirit. I don't want to be disconnected from you any longer, Lord. May my heart's cries connect us. In Your mighty name, amen.

Day 38

Walk in with Faith

When Jesus walked into Jairus' house to awaken His daughter, the Bible tells us that there was funeral music playing and a crowd making a lot of noise. Here is a little girl who Jesus said only slept, but the crowd laughed at Him because they thought she was dead. In order for Jesus to heal her, He had the doubters, the unbelievers, and the cynics leave. He knew that the environment the crowd created was made for death and not life. When they left, He told her to arise and there the girl stood. When your mother is sick and the doctor says she will be dead by tomorrow, who do you allow to come into the room with you? When you're told that your child has a disease that there is no cure for, what type of music do you begin to play? When you've lost everything you once had and you have faith that God is going to give it all back to you plus more, who do you ask to pray with you? When you are walking into the room with faith, don't invite those who will walk in with fear. When you're told that there is no cure for your child's disease, don't start creating a playlist to play at your child's funeral. Develop a playlist that honors God because He will heal your child. When the devil has stolen your joy, your happiness, and your peace of mind, don't go to someone who is going to drain you more and more, but ask someone who is filled with faith, with joy, and with peace to pray for you. Walk in the room, walk in the fire, walk on the water with faith in God and not in fear of death!

Scripture

He went inside and asked, "Why all this commotion and weeping? The child isn't dead; she's only asleep." The crowd laughed at him. But he made them all leave, and he took the girl's father and mother and his three disciples into the room where the girl was lying.

Mark 5:39-40 NLT

Prayer

No matter where I walk, I will walk in with faith. I will walk into my home with faith. I will walk into my job with faith. I will walk into my school with faith. I will walk into my marriage with faith. If I am visiting a friend or family member who may be in the hospital or at home sick, I will walk in the room with faith. There is healing power in Your name and that is where my faith lies. In Jesus name, amen.

Day 39

Pray as They Prey

Pray for those who prey on you. Pray for those who have falsely accused you. Pray for those who have persecuted you. Pray for those who have bullied you. Pray for those who laughed at you. Pray for those who doubt you. Pray for those who have tried killing you. Pray for those who have abused you. Pray for those who have used you. Pray for those who wanted to stone you. Pray for those who hate you. Jesus' greatest commandment was for you and I to love one another. How can you love someone if you don't pray for them? You may come from a family that dumped you on the street when you were a baby, but now they're coming after you for your money. Pray for them. Maybe the person who broke into your house a year ago was just released from prison today. Pray for them. Maybe the drunk driver who was involved in the hit and run that killed your child two years ago was released from prison today. Pray for them. When you realize that your best friend has been preying on you, keep on praying for them. When your spouse walks out on you for someone else, pray for them. Pray for those who many people may not be praying for. Pray for those who may be preyed upon. Even if you are the prey, you must always pray.

Scripture

But I say, love your enemies! Pray for those who persecute you!

Matthew 5:44 NLT

Prayer

I will pray for my enemies. I will pray for those who haven't found a place in their heart to forgive me. I will pray for those who have betrayed me. I will pray for those who have planned on killing me. My defense is prayer. You are my shield! No weapon formed against me shall prosper! In Jesus name, amen!

Day 40

The Mountain

Anytime there is a mountain presented to you, don't become intimidated by its presence. Don't become discouraged by the steepness of its side. The clouds may cover the peak, but that doesn't mean it's impossible for you to reach the top of the mountain. When there is a mountain in your life, view it as an opportunity for you to climb to a higher atmosphere. For those of you with asthma or have the sickle cell trait like myself, you may recall your doctor telling you that it is important for you to refrain from doing things that require you to go into a different altitude such as mountain climbing or skydiving. As true as that may be, I am not talking about climbing Mount Everest. I am referencing spiritual mountains. You may not be able to physically see these mountains, but you know you've got some climbing to do when God reveals to you that there's more to your life than working 40 hours per week. You know a mountain is present when you've been diagnosed with a disease that the doctors have no idea how to treat. You can sense a mountain's presence when you feel as if you're stuck in a place where there is little to no sunlight. What do you do when there is a mountain in your life? You must climb. I understand the rocks are unevenly edged and the wind makes the climb unsteady, but you cannot dwell in the depths of the valley. I understand climbing the mountain requires you to adapt to a new altitude. It may be difficult to breathe at first, but God will breathe life into you so that you can keep on climbing. If you're afraid of heights, God says to not fear! What are you afraid of? If God is before you who or what can be against you? As you begin to climb you'll become stronger, you'll adapt to the altitudes God has prepared for you, and you'll soon realize that this mountain was no different than a small bump in the road! When life gets difficult, you must climb! When your marriage gets tough, you must climb! When you feel healthy, but the doctor tells you you're not, you must climb! When your cross gets heavier and heavier and life continues to tear the flesh off your back, keep climbing!

Scripture

You are glorious and more majestic than the everlasting mountains.

Psalms 76:4 NLT

Prayer

The mountain that is in front of me will not stop me. You have given me the strength to climb this mountain and to reach its peak. In Jesus name, amen.

Day 41

Get Angry

When you become angry, what are you angry for? Who are you angry at? You become angry when you're lied to. You become angry when you're told the truth. You become angry when someone betrays you. You become angry when your doctor tells you you're obese. You become angry when your boyfriend or girlfriend breaks up with you. You become angry when someone curses your family out. You become angry when your name is slandered. You become angry when someone says something you don't agree with on Facebook. You become angry when your friend forgets to tag you in a photo on Instagram. You become angry when you're not invited to the party where you clearly weren't wanted. All these things cause many people to become angry, but when someone uses God's name in vain, we don't become angry. When someone talks bad about God, we don't become angry. When people give their tithes to the basketball stadium, we don't become angry. When our friends and family are fearful, we don't become angry. When someone uses God's name in vain, it should make you angry! When God is being disrespected, it should make you angry! When people are stealing from God, it should make you angry! Jesus became angry when He saw what was taking place in His Father's house! He became angry when the disciples were fearful about a temporary storm! If you don't become angry when our God is persecuted, it's time for your spirit to be checked!

Scripture

'Jesus entered the Temple and began to drive out all the people buying and selling animals for sacrifice. He knocked over the tables of the money changers and the chairs of those selling doves. He said to them, "The Scriptures declare, 'My Temple will be called a house of prayer,' but you have turned it into a den of thieves!"

Matthew 21:12-13 NLT

Prayer

Dear Lord, I won't let anyone around me use your name in vain. I won't let any of my friends or family talk recklessly about You. It makes you mad when I slander my parent's name or when others slander my name, so I should become angry when someone disrespects Your name! You have done too much for me to sit back and listen to someone disrespect You! I will no longer allow it! In Jesus name, amen.

Day 42

Attack With Prayer

When you are surrounded, threatened, or offended how do you respond? What do you do when the enemy holds a gun to your face or a sword to your neck? What do you do when the enemy has developed a nuclear weapon that can destroy a quarter of the world's population? What weapon will use when the enemy stabs you in the back? When God says attack, we must attack with prayer. When David was surrounded by the enemy, he prayed that God would deliver him from the hands of his enemy. When Shadrach, Meshach, and Abednego refused to bow down to King Nebuchadnezzar, he decided to throw them into the fire. They could've attacked him by reaching for the swords of the soldiers, but they chose to attack with prayer. When Daniel was thrown into the lion's den, he didn't attack the lions with a rock or a spear, but he attacked his situation with prayer. When the romans were nailing Jesus to the cross, He didn't call on Heaven's Armies to come save Him from the pain that was being inflicted upon Him, but He prayed for the soldiers because they had no clue what they were doing. When the enemy attacks you with a gun, you need to attack him with prayer. When the enemy attacks you with a sword, you need to attack him with prayer. When the enemy attacks you with a disease, you must attack him with prayer. Prayer is your bulletproof vest. Prayer is your shield. Prayer is your medication. If our nation along with many others realized that a spiritual warfare can only be fought with prayer and not guns, rocket launchers, or nuclear weapons, our world would be a much better place. Your weapon will run out of ammo, but you can never run out of prayer. Attack with prayer!

Scripture

'Jesus said, "Father, forgive them, for they don't know what they are doing." And the soldiers gambled for his clothes by throwing dice.

Luke 23:34 NLT

Prayer

I won't attack with flesh and blood because I will attack with prayer. I won't react by cursing out my enemy, but I will respond by praying for them. I won't hide in fear, but I will walk in faith! In Jesus name, amen.

Day 43

The Rock

Imagine how Isaac felt when his father told him that they were going to climb the mountain in search of a sacrifice. As a child, I am sure he was excited to embark on a journey with his father to provide a sacrifice for God. Abraham carried the knife while Isaac carried the wood on his back that would be used for the burnt offering. As they approached the top of the mountain, Isaac began to question why they had all the supplies for a sacrifice, but they had no sheep. Nothing made sense to Isaac until his father tied him to the rock. Think about how this made Isaac feel. He watched as his father raised the knife that would be plunged into his racing heart. In the moment when Isaac's back was against the rock and he had nowhere else to go, God revealed a lamb for Abraham to sacrifice, which ultimately saved Isaac's life. When your back is up against the rock and you have nowhere to go, always know that God will make a way. When the Israelites were traveling through the desert, God made water rush out of a rock. Christ is our cornerstone. When it seems as if we're trapped in a corner, remember that Jesus is there with you. When people want to stone you with their words, remember that Christ will deliver you from their hands. He is our foundation and our rock!

Scripture

The Lord is my rock, my fortress, and my savior; my God is my rock, in whom I find protection. He is my shield, the power that saves me, and my place of safety.

Psalms 18:2 NLT

Prayer

The wind won't be able to blow me away because You are my foundation. The rain won't be able to tear me down because You are my rock. There is nothing the enemy can throw at me that will destroy me You are my shield. I am safe because You are on my side. In Jesus name, amen.

Day 44

Definition of Happy

The definition of happy varies between each and every person. For some, happiness is being able to spend as much time as possible with their family. For others, happiness means getting paid well while doing what you love. With that being said, it is important to understand that your definition of happiness will change throughout your life. A baby is happy when it's cradled in the warmth of its mother's arms. Happiness to a child may be receiving a lot of toys for Christmas or eating as many sweets as they want without getting in trouble. Happiness to a teenager may be going to the movies with their friends or going on a date with the boy or girl they've had a crush on since elementary school. Happiness to a young adult may be getting into the college of their dreams, pursuing their calling, or starting a family. Happiness to an elderly person may be enjoying retirement while spending time with their grandkids or getting up early in the morning to have coffee with some of their lifelong friends. When you believe you can only be happy at a certain age or stage in life, you must redefine your definition of what it means to be happy. If you're not happy because you're unable to do the things that you did when you were young, before you were married, or before you got that promotion, you must find happiness in the place you are now. What makes you happy in this season may not make you happy in the next. Be open to redefining your definition of happiness!

Scripture

Always be full of joy in the Lord. I say it again—rejoice!

Philippians 4:4 NLT

Prayer

When I am sick, I will be joyful. When I am poor, I will praise You. Whether I'm single or married, I'll be happy. In the valley or on the mountaintop, I will remain joyful. You are my joy! In Jesus name, amen.

Day 45

Great, Not Famous

Many people believe that in order to be great, you must be famous or to be famous, you must be great. Our society compares fame to greatness because of the great amounts of money one may earn or the amount of attention one may receive. Yes, there are many famous people who have done great things, but if we're being honest, there are many more great people who are not famous. Think about the doctors and the nurses who spend a countless number of hours caring for our loved ones. Think about the educators who have an enormous impact on our children's lives. Think about John the Baptist. He preached a message of repentance while baptizing people all while living in the wilderness. Jesus called John the Baptist the greatest prophet to ever live, yet he wasn't famous. Will you not produce the great thing God has placed inside of you because you're not famous? Who's to say that you'll ever get famous. If your goal is to be famous, do something that doesn't matter. Start a reality T.V. show that doesn't reach those who are lost. If you want to be cool on Earth, talk and walk like everybody else. If you want to be recognized as a great man in the kingdom of Heaven, you must do what's great in

God's eyes. Choose joy over anger. Choose peace over depression. Choose greatness instead of famous.

Scripture

Do your best to present yourself to God as one approved, a worker who has no need to be ashamed, rightly handling the word of truth.

2 Timothy 2:15 NLT

Prayer

God, I want to be the greatest man or woman of God for You. I'm not worried about being famous, celebrated, or known all around the world. I want to be great in Your eyes. You see me for who I am internally, not externally. In Jesus name, amen.

Day 46

Give it to God

You will face many battles throughout life. There will be battles in your marriage, with your finances, with your family, with your health, and in your mind. As much as you may always want to be in control, you won't be. If you think you can overcome your battle alone, you can't. In order to overcome the battles that you are faced with, you must give it to God. If you've been in a battle with your marriage for 10, 15, or 20 years, it's because you haven't given your marriage to God. If you've been battling your finances, it's because you haven't given your money to God. If your family has had many battles over the years that you all just can't seem to get over, you must give your issues with one another to God. If you're battling your health after you've been taking the same medications for 20 years, you haven't given your body over to God. If the battles of your mind prevent you from going to sleep at night, you haven't given your thoughts to God. When you give your problems to God, you don't talk about them, you don't worry, you don't stress, you don't become anxious, and you don't become fearful. When you give your mind to God, you won't have suicidal thoughts. When you give your body to God, you won't have sex with every man or woman that looks pleasing to the eye. Giving your battle to God requires you to surrender unto Him. If you surrender to the enemy, he will steal your joy, destroy your mind, and will kill you. When you surrender to God, He will give you peace above all understanding. There's no reason to stress after you've given your problem to God because He will be victorious! Give it to God and go to sleep!

Scripture

Give all your worries and cares to God, for he cares about you.

1 Peter 5:7 NLT

Prayer

I lay my anxiety at Your feet. I lay my stress at Your feet. I lay my ailments at Your feet. I lay my feelings of loneliness, depression, discouragement at Your feet. I am only harming myself the longer I worry about things that are out of my control. In Jesus name, amen.

Day 47

Idols

Idols existed over 2,000 years ago and they still exist today. God was serious when He said to not worship anything or anyone else. When you think of someone worshipping other idols, you think of them bowing down or praying to a statue. You think of them singing or praying unto a god that doesn't exist. If you haven't noticed, idols are more than statues. Idols can appear in the form of an actor or actress, a singer, a musician, an athlete, or even a chief executive. You think you don't worship anything else, but you watch football more than you read your Bible. You praise your boss more than you praise God. You join the crowd in jumping and screaming at Lollapalooza, but you don't lift your hands nor sing your heart out to God at church. People cry when a celebrity touches them, but they won't cry when they hear the story about a man Who died for them. People believe in the luck of the Irish more than the promises of God. Today, I am warning you, do not put any other man, woman, child, or materialistic thing above God. They are not worth going to hell for! When you're screaming and crying at a concert that has nothing to do with God, think about who you're worshipping. God may speak through your pastor, but your pastor is not God. God may speak through the prophets, but the prophets before and the prophets today are not God! If you worship anything or anyone else but God, you are worshipping a false idol!

Scripture

You must not make for yourself an idol of any kind or an image of anything in the heavens or on the earth or in the sea.

Exodus 20:4 NLT

Prayer

God forgive me if I have worshipped anything or anyone else other than You. Forgive me if I have made an idol out of a celebrity or sport. You deserve more of my time than football, basketball, or the Avengers. You are the One and only God! You are my God. In Jesus name, amen.

Day 48

Protection

Wherever the President of the United States stands, there are secret service agents there to protect him. Wherever you see the Queen of England walking, secret agents are there to protect her. When you see celebrities such as Beyoncé or Lebron James, they usually have bodyguards to protect them. Although you don't have a physical bodyguard or secret service detail to protect you from humans that may try to harm you, God assigned angels to you the day you were born. You and I may not be able to see these angels, but they walk with us everywhere we go. They're with us in the grocery store, at the movies, at church, at the amusement park, and everywhere we go. You may not have paparazzi to worry about, but there are evil spirits who have been trying to get to you. There are evil spirits who have tried getting in your mind, but the angels won't let them touch you. There are demons driving cars that were meant to kill you, but your angels protected you. There are demonic spirits that have tried assassinating you, but your angels won't let those demons get a shot off on you. If you ever sense resistance from somebody, maybe your angels are trying to protect you. If there's a person that you find attractive and want to talk to, but you just can't seem to get to them, your angels may be trying to protect you from a spirit in that person that you cannot see. You are protected 24/7, 365 days a year. Whenever you're going through a storm, angels are with you. Angelic protection is much greater than any secret service protection! You are protected!

Scripture

For he will order his angels to protect you wherever you go.

Psalms 91:11 NLT

Prayer

Thank you Lord for sending angels to protect me. They guard me from the demons who have been assigned to kill me. They protect me from the evil spirits who want to steal my peace of mind! I am protected! Thank You, Jesus! In Your mighty name, amen.

Day 49

It Won't Be Easy

I wish I can tell you that life is easy, but it's not. It's not easy giving to other people when you have nothing. It's not easy loving people who don't love you. It's not easy lifting up other people when you have no strength to lift yourself. It's not easy to pray for those who persecute you. It's not easy to smile in front of your wife when you have no money. It's not easy to carry your child while carrying your cross. Life is not easy. I wish I could tell you that every day of your life will be joyful, but it's hard to be joyful when you have to bury your own child. I wish I could tell you that your life will be filled with love, but it's not easy loving others when you were raised in a household full of hate. I wish I could tell you that marriage is easy, but it gets tough when you and your spouse are on the edge of losing everything you own. I wish I could tell you reaching your destiny will be easy, but it's hard to press against the pressure of quitting when more people are telling you to give up rather than to keep going. Jesus knew fulfilling His purpose wouldn't be easy. I'm sure it wasn't easy knowing that the same people who screamed, "Hosanna!," would be the same people screaming, "Crucify Him!" It couldn't have been easy knowing that the one who broke bread with Him would later betray Him or the one He called His rock would deny

Him three times. It wasn't easy being nailed to the cross when He had the power to call on Heaven's Armies. Although life isn't always easy, God has given us the strength to endure every trial and tribulation. He won't put you through anything that you won't be able to handle! It's not easy, but you have the strength!

Scripture

God blesses those who patiently endure testing and temptation. Afterward they will receive the crown of life that God has promised to those who love him.

James 1:12 NLT

Prayer

Although it's not easy to spread the good news when everyone only wants to listen to the bad news, I will keep on spreading Your good word. I may be threatened or persecuted, but I know I am making You proud. As storms arise in this life, I will remain strong. When the trials seem too great, I know that You're with me. It may not be easy, but I am blessed. In Jesus name, amen.

Day 50

Peace

If you allow the devil to get in your mind, he will disrupt your peace. Anytime the enemy disrupts your peace, he has gained control of your mind. He'll disrupt your peace by stealing your joy. He'll disrupt your peace by bullying your child while they're at school. The enemy will disrupt your peace by causing you to panic when a virus is released that won't touch you or your loved ones. If you're full of anxiety, confusion, anger, hostility, stress, and depressed, you've given the enemy permission to disrupt your peace! You may be reading this today feeling like one thing happens right after another. As soon as you figure something out, the enemy slaps you with something else! It's not your job to stop the storm! It's your responsibility to remain peaceful through the storm! The only reason the enemy keeps bothering you is because he has stolen your peace. It is time for you to take back your peace today! When the enemy punches you with sickness, you'll remain peaceful. When the enemy slaps you with a pregnant teenager, you'll remain peaceful! When the enemy spits negative reports on you, you'll remain peaceful. You shall have peace above all understanding! The enemy no longer has permission to disrupt your peace! You are peaceful!

Scripture

"I am leaving you with a gift—peace of mind and heart. And the peace I give is a gift the world cannot give. So don't be troubled or afraid."

John 14:27 NLT

Prayer

God, bless me with peace above all understanding. I will be peaceful when those closest to me throw me in the pit. I will remain peaceful when others want to throw me in the fire. When all hell breaks loose, I will be at peace because You are my peace. In Jesus name, amen.

Day 51

Open Your Heart

In order to hear God, you must open your heart. In order to receive the Holy Spirit, you must open your heart. He can't bless you if your heart is closed. He can't deliver you if you won't give Him access to the place where you're in the most pain. God loves you and wants to bless you beyond measure, but you must open your heart. He wants to show you His unconditional love, but He can't if you won't open your heart. You may eat a heart-healthy diet and exercise daily, but when the doctor tells you that you need a stent to open up the arteries that are clogged, that's the unforgiveness lingering in your heart. The stent won't get rid of the unforgiveness you have against your father for walking out on you and your mother 20 years ago. Your heart won't be whole until you have forgiven your father. When your heart is racing for no reason and you begin to break out in sweats, but you have no underlying medical condition, it's because you've become anxious about something that is out of your control. Open your heart and believe that God has everything under control. He has a plan to prosper you, and not to harm you. You may have recently noticed that you have a cyanotic tone to your skin, yet your blood work revealed that there is nothing wrong with you. There may be nothing physically wrong with you, but a few years ago when your family was killed in a car accident, your heart became cold and your spirit was no longer on fire for God. If you just open your heart and give it to God again, He will give you the strength and the peace to live a faith-filled life again. Today, I want you to just open your heart to God. Let Him in.

Scripture

Trust in the Lord with all your heart; do not depend on your own understanding.

Proverbs 3:5 NLT

Prayer

I open my heart to You, Lord. Anything that is in my heart that should not be there, remove it. Any pain, unforgiveness, or anger that is poisoning my heart, God cleanse me. Renew my heart just as You have renewed my mind. In Jesus name, amen.

Day 52

When You Don't Know

It can be scary when you don't know where you're going. It's frightening when you want to take another step, but you don't know what you're going to step into. The Bible tells us to walk by faith and not by sight. If you were able to see where God is taking you, you wouldn't need faith. If God told you not only where to go, but how to get there, you wouldn't need faith during the process. Many people believe they're walking by faith when they know how to get to where they're going. They're not walking by faith. They're walking by sight. Faith is when you truly don't know. Faith is required when you don't know how you're going to get into that medical program with a 2.0 grade point average. Faith is required when you want to propose to your girlfriend of seven years, but you don't have the money to purchase a home. Your faith is tested when you see where you want to go, but you don't know how to get there. Your faith is tested when God asks you to give $100 to somebody, yet you only have $200 to your name. Your faith is tested when God asks you to give away your brand-new Mercedes to the man who you see riding his bike to work every day. Having faith is never easy. When the ground is dark and the wind is heavy, have faith in God. He won't let you stumble.

Scripture

For we walk by faith, not by sight.

2 Corinthians 5:7 NKJV

Prayer

When I don't know where to go, I will walk by faith. When I don't know how things will work out, I will keep pressing in faith. When I don't know what I am meant to do, I will seek You. I know that You are testing my faith when I truly don't know. In Jesus name, amen.

Day 53

Transitions

Transitions in life are not always easy. When you are watching a play, there is usually a blackout in between scenes. The director must transition the audience from one scene to the next. During these transitions, the living room where the characters were once sitting may now be a bedroom. The couch that was on stage left is now a tall mirror for a woman to look at while doing her make-up. Between the cast and the crew, everyone must work with one another if they want a smooth transition. When God is ready to transition you from one season to the next, expect a blackout. God thrives in the darkness. When we can't see what He's doing, that's when we should be excited about what He is preparing for us, but it's in the dark when most of us become afraid. It's during the transition when He is transforming you from the associate to the Chief Executive. It's during the transition when He transforms the way you think. People won't recognize you during the transition because they're not able to see the work that God is doing on the inside of you. When it seems like nothing is happening, God is moving! Trust Him in transition!

Scripture

This means that anyone who belongs to Christ has become a new person. The old life is gone; a new life has begun!

2 Corinthians 5:17 NLT

Prayer

God, take me out of my comfort zone. Transition me from one scene to the next. Use me in places where I never thought I would be. As you transition me from one season to the next, I know that You are developing me according to Your purpose. In Jesus name, amen.

Day 54

No Epidural

There are many moments in life where many of us wish a doctor could inject us with an epidural. The more and more we push, the greater the pain becomes. You may be trying to push through a marriage that is close to dying right before it makes it out the womb of the storm. Maybe your mind has been in labor for two years, but pushing any longer seems impossible. Someone you know may be trying to give birth to forgiveness. They want to forgive the man that molested them years ago, but the pain is too great for them to push past all of the anger and hatred they have towards that individual. When Jesus was on the cross, He was offered wine with myrrh by the Romans. Myrrh was a narcotic given to a man during crucifixion so that he would be able to endure the suffering. Jesus refused to drink this medicine that could have possibly reduced some of the pain He was experiencing because He wanted to endure the pain while simultaneously being fully conscious of everything He was experiencing. He didn't want to take any shortcuts. He knew who He was dying for and was willing to pay the ultimate price. We may not ever experience the pain and the suffering that Jesus experienced, but there will be moments in life where pushing through seems impossible. We may cry out for an epidural, but God knows it's in those moments where we become stronger. It's in those moments where we become deeply rooted in Him. There is no easy way out. A great reward lies ahead for those who continue to push through the trials and tribulations we face here on Earth.

Scripture

They offered him wine drugged with myrrh, but he refused it.

Mark 15:23 NLT

Prayer

Although the pain is great, You knew that I would be able to handle it. It may hurt when my family doesn't believe in me or my friends betray me, but I know the experiences You take me through in life will only strengthen me. I don't need an epidural because You are my pain reliever. In Jesus name, amen.

Day 55

Don't Let Education Stop You

Education doesn't define your destination. There have been many great men and women who have walked this Earth with nothing but a high school diploma, yet they've achieved more than someone with a PhD. An education didn't stop the Wright brothers from building a plane. An education didn't stop Bill Gates from developing Microsoft. An education didn't stop Bishop T.D. Jakes or Pastor Mike Todd from leading the church. An education didn't stop Kobe Bryant from publishing multiple New York Best-Sellers. Don't let your degree in health administration stop you from publishing faith-based books. Just because you didn't attend seminary doesn't disqualify you from teaching the word of God. When Jesus approached His disciples, He didn't ask what level of education they have attained. It wasn't required of Peter to attain a bachelor's degree in zoology or theology to be the fisher of fishermen. He didn't need an associate degree to be called Jesus' rock. When you want to fulfill the will God has for your life, God's only requirement is for you to trust Him. Trust Him in the seasons where there is little to no rain. Trust Him when everyone tells you that you're not qualified. When you're qualified by God, nobody can disqualify you. His YES is greater than any man's no. When you have an eighth-grade education and God tells you that you will be one of the greatest leaders this world has ever seen, will you continue to go after your destiny or will you let the opinions of others stop you? If you're reading this today, I want to remind you that God has a purpose for you!

Scripture

It is not that we think we are qualified to do anything on our own. Our qualification comes from God.

2 Corinthians 3:5 NLT

Prayer

I may not have a high school diploma, but that won't stop me from seeking Your will for my life. I may not have a college degree, but that doesn't limit the degree in which I will succeed. You will take me to places that no degree could ever take me. You can teach me more in one day than one may learn in four years. You are my Professor. In Jesus name, amen.

Day 56

What if...

When you begin to run after your destiny, there will always be the temptation of "what if..." What if I start my race, but I'm not able to finish? What if I give birth to the thing God has impregnated me with, but I'm not able to raise it? What if I publish the book, but nobody reads it? What if I take my shot at the woman of my dreams, but she rejects me? What if nobody ever loves me? What if I fail along the way? The list of, "What if," will forever follow you. If you quit today because other people keep saying what if what if what if, tomorrow, those same people will be saying what if you kept on going? What if you kept on pushing? Where would you be today? If you quit today, you'll spend the rest of your life singing what if. If you turn around as you approach the end of the road, you'll die wondering, "What if I would've kept on walking?" If you become fearful of jumping because you can't see the wings God has given you to fly, you'll always think, "What if I would've jumped although I didn't have the strength to fly?" If you're reading this today, stop thinking about all of the negative things that can happen. Stop making decisions based on what you see. Stop thinking about death when God has given you life. What if you change the way you think today? Think about where you'll be tomorrow, next week, next month, or next year. If God can split the Red Sea for the Israelites to walk through, He will make a way for you even if it appears to be a dead end.

Scripture

For as he thinks in his heart, so is he.

Proverbs 23:7 NKJV

Prayer

I will no longer say "What if." I will not doubt You. I will no longer ponder on the negative things that may never happen. All things are possible through Christ. In Jesus name, amen.

Day 57

Own Your Mountain

What makes achievers different from dreamers? They keep pressing in the face of adversity. Instead of crying and whining about not having an education or enough money to climb, they become resourceful and use whatever God has equipped them with. Those who have made an impact today didn't dwell in the puddle of discouragement. They didn't let one mistake stop them from believing who they are and what they could achieve. In order to be effective, you must own your mountain and everything you encounter while climbing. During your climb, you must not be afraid of missing a step or not knowing where to go next. Rocks may fall and the rain may pour, but don't let anything or anyone cause you to loosen your grip on what God has placed in your hands. We're not perfect. God knew that you would make mistakes along the way, but that didn't stop Him from placing that gift in your hand. He gave it to you because He trusts you. Own your mountain. It's worth the climb.

Scripture

God is our refuge and strength, A very present help in trouble. Therefore we will not fear, even though the earth be removed, and though the mountains be carried into the midst of the sea; Though its waters roar and be troubled, though the mountains shake with its swelling.

Psalms 46:1-3 NKJV

Prayer

Jesus, you said that if I have faith as small as a mustard seed, I can move mountains! The mountain that is in front me will not stop me. It may stand tall and look wide, but there is no mountain too great for me because You are in me. I will own my mountains! In Jesus name, amen.

Day 58

The Enemy's Opportunity

Don't give the enemy opportunities to destroy you. Everything that comes to mind doesn't have to come out of your mouth. The Bible tells us that our tongues are the greatest of all weapons. It is our responsibility to filter what comes out of our mouths. The devil can't read your mind, but once you have spoken about what you were thinking, you now give the enemy the opportunity to play with your words. When you speak death instead of life, the enemy will use those words to destroy your mind. He will use those words to steal your peace and joy. He will use those words to kill you by causing you to think that you're worthless and that you have no purpose in this life. The enemy is after your mind! Your words will either give him the opportunity to get into your head or they will force him to leave you and everything you possess. Be mindful of what you speak!

Scripture

Death and life are in the power of the tongue, and those who love it will eat its fruit.

Proverbs 18:21 NKJV

Prayer

I won't give the enemy an opportunity to kill me with my own words. I won't speak death. I won't speak negatively. I won't curse others. I won't speak sexually. I will speak as if I were speaking with You. Control my tongue, Lord. In Jesus name, amen.

Day 59

Love God

Many people today have fallen in love with church, but fell out of love with God. They love their pastor, a couple of singers from the choir, an elder or two, and their seat more than they love God. The place that was meant to worship God is abused. Some people clap for the pastor more than they clap for God. They raise their hands for the person holding the mic, not God. There are people today who speak to their pastor before they speak to God. Today, some people confess their sins to man before they confess to God. Maybe you've become discouraged because someone has broken a promise that you've been standing on. I want to remind you that you are to stand on the promises of God! No matter what season you may be in, no matter how much money you have, God's promises will always stand! Stop giving your body to someone who only wants you for a quick minute. Stop trying to hide under someone who can never cover your sins. Stop crying and begging for someone to forgive you. They are not God! God loves you whether you're clothed or naked. He has covered your sins with His blood! Once you ask Him to forgive you, He remembers no more! God won't hold a grudge against you. He won't expose you just to dispose of you. God loves you. He wants you to reciprocate that love. When you're singing, remember you're worshipping God. When you're crying, cry your heart out to God! Love God first!

Scripture

But seek first the kingdom of God and His righteousness, and all these things shall be added to you.

Matthew 6:33 NKJV

Prayer

I am in love with you, Jesus. I am not in love with the choir at my church or the theatrics of my pastor's sermon. God, I am in love with you and your message. I love you, Jesus. In Your mighty name, amen.

Day 60

Let Them Go

Either you or somebody you know has a hard time letting people go. They're afraid of being alone. They worry if anybody will ever love them again. Maybe the man who you thought was your husband left you for another woman. Maybe the woman you were planning on proposing to next week has been on the phone with some guy for the past 2 weeks every night past 1 a.m. Maybe the employee of the year just put in their two weeks and you don't know if you'll ever to be able to replace them. Maybe a member of your church was offended that you didn't recognize them, and they sent you an email explaining that they no longer plan on attending your services. All of us at some point in time have come across people who will either tell us they want to go or they're actions prove that they don't want to stay. When people want to leave you or your business, LET THEM GO! If you're on the phone and the person doesn't seem interested in you or anything you're saying, tell them to have a good night and MOVE ON! If an employee wants to leave because another company has offered them more money, don't beg them to stay, let them go! Many people have a hard time letting people go. They feel bad for telling somebody good-bye. When Jesus revealed that Judas would be the one to betray Him, He didn't beg Judas to stay. He didn't complain about it nor did He make Judas feel guilty. Jesus told Judas to go and do what he must. Jesus knew that Judas served his purpose in life. There was no reason for Jesus to keep Judas around any longer! It was time to let Judas go! There will be people who are seasonal and there will be people who are permanent. Don't make a seasonal person permanent. If they were meant to only be with you in the winter, don't be shocked when they melt in the summer. Let them go!

Scripture

When Judas had eaten the bread, Satan entered into him. Then Jesus told him, "Hurry and do what you're going to do."

John 13:27 NLT

Prayer

I choose to let go of the people that only tolerate me. I choose to let go of those who aren't contributing to my future. God, give me the discernment to let someone go after they have served their purpose. In Jesus name, amen.

Day 61
Rely On God

When we've worked with someone our entire lives or grew up with someone who was always complimenting us, it becomes easy to rely on people. When someone has always been available to help us, we start to think that people are always reliable. The truth is, the closer you get to your destiny, the more people will let you down. When we're going after something that others don't see, you'll soon discover that you won't receive the support you expected. When you look to others for validation, you won't ever reach your destination. You must always rely on God. God will open up doors that other men tried to close. He will promote you when other people demote you. He invested in you before your mother gave birth to you. If God created you, that means He invested in everything that He gave you the ability to do. Don't let a rich man stop you from pursuing your wealthy dreams. You don't need any person's money or time. All you need is God! He will introduce you to the men and women that will support you. He will connect you to the men and women that will be willing to invest in the vision He has given you! When you rely on God and not on man, watch miraculous things appear all around you!

Scripture

And my God shall supply all your need according to His riches in glory by Christ Jesus.

Philippians 4:19 NKJV

Prayer

Lord, You are all I need. I lean on You for understanding, wisdom, knowledge, and strength. When I lean on You, I am at peace. When I lean on You, I remember that I have a purpose. In the times where I may be in trouble, I will lean on You. In Jesus name, amen.

Day 62

Who is your Simon?

As Jesus became weaker and the cross became heavier, the soldiers began to realize that He wouldn't be able to travel much further alone. A man from Cyrene named Simon was called upon to help Jesus carry the cross. The Bible briefly mentions Simon, but this man plays a significant role in Jesus' story. He represents a person who is willing to help you when life has beaten you to the core. When your beard is ripped off and your back is exposed and everyone is screaming, "Crucify you," Simon is the person who will step in when the weight of the cross begins to get too heavy. Simon is the person who will bless a family with food when they barely have enough to get by. Simon is the person who will pay for your groceries when you barely had enough. Simon is the individual who will lift you up when everybody else is kicking you down. You may be reading this today and have yet to meet your Simon, but I want you to know that God will send someone to help you right on time. Maybe God has called you to be somebody else's Simon. If you know a family who is about to be evicted out of their home or a young adult who is on the border of dropping out of college because the financial burden has become too heavy for them or their family to carry, I want you to stand up and be their Simon today!

Scripture

Along the way, they came across a man named Simon, who was from Cyrene, and the soldiers forced him to carry Jesus' cross.

Matthew 27:32 NLT

Prayer

Reveal my Simon to me, Lord. The person who will carry the cross with me when it gets heavy. The person who won't leave me hanging while everybody is throwing rocks at me and spitting on me. In Jesus name, amen.

Day 63

Bless Somebody

Our generation and generations before us tend to overindulge materialistic items. Whether it be a closet full of shoes or a drawer full of watches, we all have things that we necessarily don't need. Maybe you have 10 pairs of basketball shoes sitting in your closet while someone you know is in desperate need of shoes. The question I have for you today is what stops you from giving away a pair of shoes that you may only wear once or twice a year? What does it take for you to bless somebody in need with something you don't need? Many people today won't give money to an organization or to another person who is in need simply because they think about when and where that money can be used for themselves. Will God not provide? The Bible says He provides for the birds in the air and the flowers on the ground. If he provides for them and we're His greatest creation, what makes you think He won't provide for you? When God has blessed you with an abundance whether it be food, clothes, or money, it's not for you to show off on social media. God has blessed you so that He can use you as a vessel to bless someone else. Today, I challenge you to bless somebody without telling the entire world what you did. You don't have to share your good deeds with social media. When you bless somebody in private, God will bless you in public.

Scripture

When you give to someone in need, don't do as the hypocrites do—blowing trumpets in the synagogues and streets to call attention to their acts of charity! I tell you the truth, they have received all the reward they will ever get. But when you give to someone in need, don't let your left hand know what your right hand is doing. Give your gifts in private, and your Father, who sees everything, will reward you.

Matthew 6:2-4 NLT

Prayer

From here on out, I vow to bless somebody else when You bless me. Just as I give unto You, I will give unto others. When someone needs clothes, I will clothe them. When someone needs food, I will feed them. When someone needs a roof over their head, I will house them. When You call me to bless somebody else, I will be obedient. In Jesus name, amen.

Day 64

The Man, Not the Gift

If the Pharisees would've recognized the Man, instead of becoming envious of His gifts, they would have never killed Him. If Satan would've recognized Who Jesus was instead of the miracles He was performing, he would've prevented the romans from killing the Son of God. Have you ever recognized a person for their gift instead of who they are? Millions of people around the world recognize Lebron James as one of the greatest players to ever play the game of basketball, but they tend to look past the man who blessed the community he grew up in with a school that guarantees its students a full-ride scholarship to college. We saw Kobe Bryant for the five championships he brought to L.A., but we didn't realize how much he enjoyed being with his family and the stories he wrote for the younger generation to read today until he passed. The reason so many celebrities become depressed today is because millions of people see their gift, but they don't see the individual struggling with mental or physical health. They see the multi-million-dollar home with the Lamborghini in the driveway, but they don't see the person in the house crying, wishing that people would see them and not only their gift. While many praise the gift, the enemy is plotting to kill the individual. It's okay to see the gift, but don't look past the man.

Scripture

But I, the Lord, search all hearts and examine secret motives. I give all people their due rewards, according to what their actions deserve.

Jeremiah 17:10 NLT

Prayer

Dear God, help me see someone for who they are and not what they do. Help me see their heart and not their skills. I want to see people just as You see them. In Jesus name, amen.

Day 65

Paralyzed

Do you have a vision? Where do you see yourself 10 years from now? What sacrifices are you willing to make to get there? How do you plan on getting there if you are mentally paralyzed? Many people see where they want to go, but can never get there because their mind is paralyzed. You believe that you are too young or too old to accomplish anything significant in life. You tell yourself that you don't have the money or the education to even start what God has revealed to you. You think that what you envision is only a thought when God is trying to tell you that can be your reality. You must activate your mind. Begin to read, be creative, write down your plan, write down what you want to achieve and when you want to achieve it. You are not where you are today because of your age, financial status, or level of education. Where you are today is because of your mind! Your mind is your roadblock. You want to run after your dreams, but you don't have the faith to stand. You want to be a leader, but you only see yourself as an ordinary person. You want a house with a three-car garage and a pool in the backyard, but you see no way out of your one-bedroom apartment. If you want to change the way you think, surround yourself with people who are smarter than you. If you know somebody who is doing today what you see yourself doing a few years from now, ask them questions. Ask them what it took, what books they read, where they invested their money. You have what it takes to get to your destination. You are capable of achieving every single one of your dreams. You must have faith in God and faith in who He created you to be. You are no longer paralyzed! Stand and get to running after your destiny.

Scripture

For God has not given us a spirit of fear and timidity, but of power, love, and self-discipline.

2 Timothy 1:7 NLT

Prayer

I am no longer paralyzed! When the enemy thought I was down and out, I stood up. When the enemy thought I could go no further, I kept on going. Just as when I was about to lose my mind, You gave me the strength to get a hold of it. I am alive and not paralyzed! In Jesus name, amen.

Day 66
Called

Are you doing what you've always wanted to do or what you were called to do? Are you a rapper when you were called to be a pastor? Are you an actor when you were called to be a teacher? Are you a construction worker when you were called to be a doctor? Whatever you may be doing today, do you feel in your heart that's where God has called you? Maybe you've always wanted to live in Los Angeles, but God has called you to live in Denver. Yes, it may be cold in Denver and the altitude is higher which makes it a little more difficult to breathe, but maybe there's a person there that God wanted you to mentor. Maybe you have always wanted to be an actor or actress because of the fame, the money, and the other celebrities you will most likely get to work with, but maybe God has called you to be a teacher because He knows the effect you'll have on a child's life. When God calls you to a place, He plans on using you there. When He calls you to a household, He plans on using you to answer someone's prayer. When He calls you to a school, He plans on using you to guide one or many of His children in the right direction. The number of people who may not know God or haven't accepted Jesus as their Lord and savior is still too many. As God's children, it is our duty to go where there is spiritual warfare. He introduced you to that teenager because they were molested when they were seven and eight years old. He introduced you to that drug addict because He knew you would have a greater impact on them than the needles they are sticking themselves with every day. You have been called! Now go fulfill His will!

Scripture

And we know that God causes everything to work together for the good of those who love God and are called according to his purpose for them.

Romans 8:28 NLT

Prayer

When You call me, I will answer. I will go where You want me to go. I will pray for the person You told me to pray for. I will stand where You have called me to stand. In Jesus name, amen.

Day 67

Out of the Grave

Have you ever been buried? Have you ever felt like you were put into a coffin that you could barely move in? Do you feel like you're in a place today where there is only death and no life? Today, I want to tell you that it is time to come out of the grave. If you've been buried in depression, it's time for you to resurrect out the grave of depression. If you've been buried in sickness, it's time for you to resurrect out the grave of your illness. If you've been buried in poverty, it's time for you to resurrect out the grave of your ill environment. If you've been buried in betrayal, you shall resurrect out the grave of distrust. If you've been buried in darkness, it's time for you to resurrect into the light. If you've been buried in discouragement, your courage shall resurrect. If you've been buried in death, today you will come back to life. The enemy will try to bury you in a place of death. A place where you can't fulfill the will of God. But Jesus proved that you and I have the power to resurrect out of our graves. Death can't hold us anymore! When the enemy picks up his shovel, you need to pick up your Bible. You will not be buried any longer. Come out of the grave, wipe the dirt off your face, put on some new clothes, and walk into life!

Scripture

And God will raise us from the dead by his power, just as he raised our Lord from the dead.

1 Corinthians 6:14 NLT

Prayer

My mind is out of the grave! My finances are out of the grave! My vision is out of the grave! You have given me new life! I will defeat debt just like you defeated death! I am no longer in debt financially, physically, or mentally! I am out of the grave! In Jesus name, amen.

Day 68

Normal

What is normal? What makes a person normal? It's normal for somebody to work 40 hours a week. It's normal for people to eat 3 meals a day. It's normal to take a shower at least once a day. It was normal for the Wright brothers to build a machine that would give them the ability to fly with eagles while others probably thought they were crazy. It was normal for Bill Gates to think of a device that would allow us to retrieve worldwide information in a matter of seconds while his colleagues thought he was some guy who was thinking of the impossible. The Wright brothers and Bill Gates proved that when you work on something that others may not see as normal, you can be successful. Going to a job that you don't love may be normal for billions of people all around the world including your family, but that doesn't have to be your norm. Your normality is your creativity. It should include who you strive to become and what you strive to achieve. You're not weird for wanting to do more in life. You're not crazy for wanting to develop something that no other man or woman has thought of. Continue to be who God has created you to be and use what He has given you. Your normality can change the future for the better.

Scripture

If your gift is to encourage others, be encouraging. If it is giving, give generously. If God has given you leadership ability, take the responsibility seriously. And if you have a gift for showing kindness to others, do it gladly. In his grace, God has given us different gifts for doing certain things well. So if God has given you the ability to prophesy, speak out with as much faith as God has given you. If your gift is serving others, serve them well. If you are a teacher, teach well.

Romans 12:6-8 NLT

Prayer

What makes You so unique, Lord, is that anything and everything You do is never normal. You perform miracles when I think it is impossible. You breathe life into me just as I think I am about to die. You are not normal, You are amazing! In Jesus name, amen.

Day 69

The Box

Have you ever tried picking up a box that was a lot heavier than it appeared? Maybe you couldn't get a firm grip or there was nobody else around to help you. After concluding that the box is too heavy to carry, you try pushing it. You put all of your weight into the box, but you still can't get the box to move. Maybe this box is the group of friends you hang around who trap you in the way you think. The box can be a class that seems to be in the way of your degree. Maybe the box is the amount of money you have in your bank account. When you believe that you don't have the strength to get around the box, it has become the roadblock to your destiny. Whatever your box may be, you have a choice to make. You will either allow the box to trap you or you will use the box as a steppingstone. When challenges arise, embrace them. When doors open, walk through them. When it's time to let people go, let them go. If you know that a box is too heavy to carry, then it's strong enough for you to step on. Whether you have to climb or jump, the box shouldn't stop you from reaching your destiny. Are you going to allow the heavy burdens in life trap you or are you going to stand tall and walk over them to get to the place God has prepared for you? You choose what you want to do with the box. Nobody else can choose for you.

Scripture

God says, "Rebuild the road! Clear away the rocks and stones so my people can return from captivity."

Isaiah 57:14 NLT

Prayer

I will no longer be trapped in a box! Whether that box is my mind or my finances, it will no longer stop me from moving forward! The box won't stop me from entering doors You have opened. In Jesus name, amen.

Day 70

Strengthen Your Grip

When you truly want something in life, you won't loosen your grip on it. The reason you haven't reached your dreams is because you didn't hold on tight enough. You didn't hold onto that idea, that work ethic, that desire to be different. Somewhere along the road your hands started to cramp and became sweaty to the point where you didn't know how much longer you would be able to hold on. People quit because they never took the time to strengthen their grip. Their grip on their marriage was weak. Their grip on their dreams were weak. Their grip on their children were weak. Their grip on their mind was weak. What you must realize is that if you don't strengthen your grip, the devil will get a grip of you. The enemy will start to tug on your mind, your finances, your family. Before you let go, I want you to think about everything you're giving up. When you become weak and discouraged, instead of looking back to see how far you've come, I want you to start looking ahead to see how close you are to reaching your destiny. When God takes you through the fire, He is strengthening your grip. When rowing your boat seems close to impossible in the midst of the storm, strengthen your grip and keep on rowing.

You are that much closer! Don't let the waves take you out! You can and you will make it through! All you have to do is strengthen your grip!

Scripture

That's right. Because I, your God, have a firm grip on you and I'm not letting go. I'm telling you, 'Don't panic. I'm right here to help you.'

Isaiah 41:13 MSG

Prayer

Thank You, Lord, for never loosening your grip on me. Thank You for holding me close. When the devil was tugging at me, You never let go of me. I want to ask You today to help strengthen my grip on the things and people I should not let go. I will hold onto love and not hate. I will grip forgiveness while I let go of anything that may be harming me. I will hold Your hand because I know that You will never let go of mine. In Jesus name, amen.

Day 71

Demand What's Yours

When the enemy is sitting in your seat, tell him to get up! When the enemy is laying in your bed, tell him to get out of your room! When the enemy is lingering around your job, kick him out! When the enemy is holding your joy, your peace, and your mind, take it all back! You must demand what is yours! Don't approach the enemy as if what he's holding was already his. Don't ask him for anything that you own. Snatch it out of his hands. I'm sure when Jesus went to hell to take the keys of death from Satan, He didn't ask politely. He reached out His hand and took from Satan what he no longer had any control over. Jesus demanded what He rightfully owned. Take back your peace! Take back your joy! Take back your mind! Take back your vision! Take back those ideas that are going to take you to another place! Take back your family! Take back your marriage! Take back your job! If you are tired of the enemy sticking his hands in everything you own, demand him to leave today!

Scripture

I am the living one. I died, but look—I am alive forever and ever! And I hold the keys of death and the grave.

Revelation 1:18 NLT

Prayer

I own my joy! I own my peace! I own my mind! I won't allow the devil to steal what God has given me. I won't allow him to sit in the seat that God made for me to sit on. I won't allow him to stand in the place where I have planted many seeds. I rebuke Satan and all of his demons! In Jesus name, amen.

Day 72

You're Breaking Out

It is time for you to break out of the prison you've been held captive in for the past 10, 20, or 30 years. The place where the enemy thought he could hold you forever will hold you no longer. If the enemy arrested your mind, you're about to break out of depression. If the enemy arrested your heart, you're about to break out of anger. If the enemy arrested your finances, you're about to break out of poverty. The enemy thought he could arrest the thought of Jesus by burying Him in a tomb. The enemy had no idea who he was messing with because no grave could hold the Son of Man. Jesus broke out of what was intended to hold Him captive. You can break away from drugs, alcohol, lust, and be free. You don't have to sit in that imaginary cell forever. You can stand up and walk away. The chains that are wrapped around your hands, your feet, and your mind are all broken! If you're reading this today and have felt like you've been imprisoned and can see little to no sunlight in your future, the devil has gotten a hold of your mind! You have been set free! Break out of the prison of death and start walking on the journey to life!

Scripture

Around midnight Paul and Silas were praying and singing hymns to God, and the other prisoners were listening. Suddenly, there was a massive earthquake, and the prison was shaken to its foundations. All the doors immediately flew open, and the chains of every prisoner fell off!

Acts of the Apostles 16:25-26 NLT

Prayer

I will no longer allow my mind to imprison me. I will not allow negative words to stop me. Today, I am breaking out of depression. I am breaking out of poverty. I am breaking out of unforgiveness. I am breaking out of lost hope. Every chain that was once on me is now broken! In Jesus name, amen.

Day 73

The Pain of Effort

There are two types of pain. The first is the pain of giving up or never fulfilling your purpose. This type of pain doesn't build you, but it can possibly kill you. This is the type of pain that won't ever leave you because you never discovered the strength you had to reach the peak of your mountain. The pain of giving up doesn't only affect you, but it may also affect the life of others. If God called you to be a game changer and you never attempted to step out on the court, the game will always remain the same. If you never fulfilled your purpose because you thought it was too late or you didn't have enough money, you can never influence the people God intended for you to have an impact on. But there is another type of pain that few successfully go through. That is the pain of effort. The pain of effort makes you stronger. It makes you wiser. Effort's pain is affiliated with many trials that will lead you to your destination. The pain of effort doesn't produce quick results, but everlasting progress. Effort's pain will encourage you to keep on going no matter how heavy the wind may get. It will encourage you to keep on pressing against the pressure of quitting. The pain of effort will give you the ability to knock down any giant that stands in front of you. If you haven't yet, I want you to experience the pain of effort. Put some effort into your marriage. Put some effort into your mind. Put some effort into your soul. The pain yields great results!

Scripture

Lazy people want much but get little, but those who work hard will prosper.

Proverbs 13:4 NLT

Prayer

While the pain of my effort is great, I know that it will produce great results. If I put forth little effort, I will see little to no results, but if I work hard for what You have for me, I will prosper like never before. You're allowing me to go through this pain because it will strengthen me. The strength I will gain from the pain of my efforts will allow me to withstand the trials and tribulations of my destiny. I am strong! I am courageous! I am willful! In Jesus name, amen.

Day 74

God's Tap

When there is someone who blew up overnight whether it be an author, artist, athlete, or musician, it's easy to think about who they met or what they did to get there. You might think about how many years they put into their craft or how much money they invested in their dream. Although these are valid reasons for one to achieve great success, they're not the reason. The reason someone appears out of what seems to be nowhere is because God has tapped them. When God knows that you're ready for the place He has prepared for you, all He has to do is tap you for the world to see you. There is no spotlight required nor any microphone needed for God to tap you. The Bible tells us that faith without works is dead. You may have the faith, but if you're not putting in the work, God won't tap you. You may be working your butt off, but if you don't have the faith, God won't tap your work. His tap will blow you up much faster than any steroid or supplement. God's tap will give you the strength to not only walk into your destiny, but to stay there. You want to be tapped by God, not by man.

Scripture

You will enjoy the fruit of your labor. How joyful and prosperous you will be!

Psalms 128:2 NLT

Prayer

The tap of Your finger will take me much further and higher than any marketing material, any amount of money, or any man's recognition. In Jesus name, amen.

Day 75

Love What You Do

Every morning when you wake up, you should be excited to get to work. Whatever you do should make you excited. You shouldn't be looking forward to the weekend or to your next vacation. Every day your goal should be to somehow make a difference while doing what you love. Who can you help? Who can you teach? Who can you train? What impact will you make today? Ask yourself what you can do to be better. Obtain books that will equip you with knowledge to help you perform on a different level (like this one). Seek mentors who will train you up in the right direction to be effective. If you have no desire to do any of these things or you dread going to work, you don't love what you do. If you don't care about becoming knowledgeable for you and the well-being of others, your job isn't important to you. Take my advice and find something else to do. What makes you happy? What do you love to do? I'm sure you just answered those questions in your head and now I want you to go after that vision. Stop thinking about what your parents and your friends think. At the end of the day, you have to do what makes you happy. I want you to be successful. I want you to be effective. I want you to look forward to work. I want you to love what you do.

Scripture

For I can do everything through Christ, who gives me strength.

Philippians 4:13 NLT

Prayer

God I want to make a difference. I want to look forward to impacting someone's life every day. It doesn't matter what my family thinks or what my friends suggest I should do. I want to do what You have called me to do. Let your purpose for my life be fulfilled. In Jesus name, amen.

Day 76

Change Your Method

It can be frustrating when we have a plan that appears to be just right, but we get nothing for it. One may become frustrated when the method their business used 20 years ago doesn't work today. Our methods cannot remain the same. You can't expect different results if you never took the time to change your methods. If you want to reach a larger audience, you can't use the same method you used when your target audience consisted of your mama, your grandmama, and your siblings. If a college athlete wants to become a professional athlete, they can't train the way they did in college and expect to be successful. They must change their method. Jesus knew the importance of changing one's methods. When Jesus saw His disciples fishing out in the sea one day, He asked if they had caught any fish and the disciples replied, "No." Now I am sure they were frustrated and just about ready to give up, but Jesus knew their method of fishing had not changed. So, He told them to throw their net on the right-hand side of the boat. I'm sure at first, the disciples were thinking, "Who is this guy and what does he know," but when they changed their methods as the teacher had instructed them to, they didn't have the strength to pull the net back into their boat because there were so many fish in it. God will tell you to change your method because He knows the blessing you've been working so hard for is on the other side of the boat. Instead of thinking your method is the only one that will ever work, start seeking God for His method. As times change and technology advances, He will give you and your business methods that will keep you above the water. I want to challenge you today to change your method in any area of your life where your methods are old and expired.

Scripture

Then he said, "Throw out your net on the right-hand side of the boat, and you'll get some!" So they did, and they couldn't haul in the net because there were so many fish in it.

John 21:6 NLT

Prayer

Lord, forgive me if my methods have been the same. Today, I am asking for Your help. I need you Jesus. I will no longer do things my way. I shall only do what is pleasing to You. In Jesus name, amen.

Day 77

Infected

Have you ever been infected before? Maybe you were infected with a cold or the flu. Maybe you developed an ear infection or an infection from an open wound. While infectious diseases can be harmful and sometimes life-threatening, there are people in your life who have attached themselves to you that are infectious. They are infected with hate, anger, unforgiveness, greed, and bitterness. It doesn't matter where you go or what you do, there's always someone around who is infected with death. I want to encourage you today to be mindful of these infected individuals. It's okay to love and pray for them, but be careful that they don't attach themselves to you. If you find yourself talking out of fear instead of faith, a fearful person has infected you. If you find yourself becoming irritable with every person that tries to talk to you, you've been infected with irritability. If you think about the worst thing that can happen in every situation, someone has infected you with negativity. If there is someone in your life, whether it be a friend or a family member, and they're infected, let them know that you love them, but you won't let that spirit of fear, hatred, anger, or bitterness get on you. Your faith should scare them away. Your joy should keep them at a distance. You will not be infected anymore! Today, you are clean!

Scripture

Don't be fooled by those who say such things, for "bad company corrupts good character."

1 Corinthians 15:33 NLT

Prayer

I will not be infected with fear, but I will be filled with faith. I will not be infected with anger, but I will be filled with forgiveness. I will not be infected with anxiety, but I will be filled with peace. In Jesus name, amen.

Day 78

Shattered

If you have ever been shattered before, you know it is not a comfortable place to be. There are pieces of you all over the place and you don't even know where to start picking yourself up. A shattered person may fear getting into another relationship because they don't want to cut the other person with a piece of themself that hasn't been glued back together. When one is shattered, it is difficult to look at themselves in the mirror because all they see is brokenness. If you're reading this today and you're shattered, I want to remind you that God reveals His gems in brokenness. God breaks us to help us, not to harm us. There is new life when we're broken. Instead of wasting time trying to pick up the pieces that are on the ground, get a broom, sweep it up, and throw it in the trash. God broke you to propel you. That diamond inside of you wouldn't be shining today if He didn't remove that boyfriend or girlfriend that was causing you more harm than good. It wouldn't be shining if you would have never failed out of that program. It wouldn't be shining if you didn't give yourself to Him. You are whole again! You are one again! You are loved and no longer shattered!

Scripture

When the man saw that he would not win the match, he touched Jacob's hip and wrenched it out of its socket.

Genesis 32:25 NLT

Prayer

God, I know You didn't break me to harm me. You broke me to propel me. You knew that the only way I would ever see what You planted on the inside of me is if you broke me. Although I may have felt shattered, You really made me whole. Thank you Jesus. In Your mighty name, amen.

Day 79

Prophesy

Did you know that you have the power to prophesy over your own life? Jesus tells us in Matthew that if we have just a little bit of faith, we can tell a mountain to move and it will move. If you have the power to tell a mountain to move, you have the power to speak healing over your life. You have the power to speak life into your marriage. You have the power to prophesy that you will come out of your financial crisis tomorrow! You see not only what you think, but what you speak. If you say, "I'm never going to get out of this community," you'll be in that same community until the day you die. If you prophesy that you will not be in the same environment you were born into, God will take you to a place beyond your imagination. Your tongue has power. It is greater than any other weapon! Use it to your advantage!

Scripture

"You don't have enough faith," Jesus told them. "I tell you the truth, if you had faith even as small as a mustard seed, you could say to this mountain, 'Move from here to there,' and it would move. Nothing would be impossible."

Matthew 17:20 NLT

Prayer

You've given me the power to speak things into existence. If I tell a mountain to move, it will move. If I say that I will defeat a giant, You will equip me to take that giant down. If I wish to see a shift in my life, I must speak good things into existence. I will no longer be in debt! Any trial You put me through shall not kill me. I am stronger! I am wiser! In Jesus name, amen.

Day 80

Throwing Shade

We live in a society where people always want to throw shade at one another. If you're reading this today and you've never heard of the phrase "throw shade," it simply means to criticize someone else. Maybe someone who was jealous of you and everything you've achieved has thrown shade at you because they don't have what you worked hard for. Those individuals who were once your friends threw shade at you for wanting to be different and not always wanting to fit in with the crowd. The only reason people want to throw shade at you is because you're shining. If you weren't shining, they would have no reason to try and cover you up. If you weren't on your way to a greater place, they wouldn't have any reason to try to bring you down. If you weren't destined to be great, they wouldn't try to make you feel inferior to them. God wants to shine through you. As you continue to give God glory for everything He has done for you, He will continue to bless you with more than you can ever imagine. No matter how much shade people may try to throw at you, they'll never be able to dim the light that is within you.

Scripture

Surely resentment destroys the fool, and jealousy kills the simple.

Job 5:2 NLT

Prayer

No matter how much shade others may try to show at me, they can never cover the light You have put inside of me. No matter how much they may try to shame me, I know You will forever love me. I will not submit to their words or their beliefs. I will remain faithful because You have never and will never break Your promises. In Jesus name, amen.

Day 81

Just Listen

The Bible tells us that out of the abundance of the heart the mouth speaks. This simply means that anything that comes out of our mouths is in our hearts. When someone is full of fear, they always talk about what they're afraid of. When someone is full of hate, you will always hear them talking about how much they can't stand this person and why they don't like another. A greedy person always talks about how an idea will benefit themselves rather than other people. On the other hand, a faithful person will speak life into their situation. A person who is full of forgiveness won't talk about what their loved ones did to them in the past and how much it hurt them because they have forgiven them. A person who is full of love will speak with kindness and patience. You don't need to be a cardiothoracic surgeon or a cardiologists to see what someone's heart is full of. The words they speak were once in their heart.

Scripture

For out of the abundance of the heart the mouth speaks.
Matthew 12:34 NKJV

Prayer

I will train my ears to listen for Your voice instead of the enemy's. I know that I don't have to do much talking to get to know someone because how they feel on the inside is what they'll speak on the outside. Just as Your word says, I will be quick to listen and slow to speak. In Jesus name, amen.

Day 82

Do Not Compromise

When the rain is getting heavier and the thunder is getting louder, the enemy will try to make a bargain with you. Satan will try to cut you a deal that sounds pleasing to the ear, but is harmful to your soul. Whatever you may be going through, don't compromise your faith. There is a rainbow on the other side of the storm. There is healing and restoration on the other side of your pain. Where you were once weak, you will now be strong. Where you couldn't stand, you will run. Where you were once blind, you will now see. Don't fall for the devil's shortcuts. They will only lead you to a dangerous place. Stay on God's path and He will surely make a way even when it seems like there is no way out.

Scripture

The temptations in your life are no different from what others experience. And God is faithful. He will not allow the temptation to be more than you can stand. When you are tempted, he will show you a way out so that you can endure.

1 Corinthians 10:13 NLT

Prayer

I will not compromise my faith to someone's fear. I will not compromise my peace for someone's anxiety. I will not allow one's depression to take away my joy. I will stay on the path that leads to life. While at times I may be tempted to venture off, I won't compromise my soul for the enemy's tactics. In Jesus name, amen.

Day 83

The Truth

Jesus came to speak the truth and nothing but the truth. He knew the truth would set us free. He told Peter that he would deny Him three times and He told Judas that he would be the one to betray Him. As Jesus was being questioned, He answered truthfully. He told the high priests that He would be on the right hand of God. He told Pilate that His kingdom is not of this world, but of another place. In the midst of telling the truth, He was betrayed, denied, persecuted, buried, but then He resurrected. Just as the truth set Jesus free, so shall it set you free. People won't trust you when you lie, but many won't like you if you tell the truth. When you tell someone the truth, don't do it to harm them, but to help them. While many may not want to hear the truth about themselves, it will set them free. It is better to be honest and persecuted than to be known as a liar and burn. I want to encourage you today to live a true and honest life.

Scripture

Pilate therefore said to Him, "Are You a king then?" Jesus answered, "You say rightly that I am a king. For this cause I was born, and for this cause I have come into the world, that I should bear witness to the truth. Everyone who is of the truth hears My voice."

John 18:37 NKJV

Prayer

Today, I vow to speak the truth and nothing but the truth. While the truth may be painful to hear at times, it will only help someone else or even myself. There is no room for growth in a lie. Lies only lead to other lies. You are the truth. You came to testify to the truth. That is why I am living today. That is why I have been given another chance to make it into heaven. In Jesus name, amen.

Day 84

A Sip

When you want a taste of what God has in store for you, He'll give you a sip, that's it. When Joseph had the dream about the sun, the moon, and the stars bowing down to him, God didn't reveal the well his brothers would dump him in or the cell he would be sleeping in for a crime he never committed. When Jesus told Peter the kind of death he would have, He didn't reveal to him that he would be hung on a cross upside down. God doesn't give you a sip to tease you, but to strengthen your faith. Peter didn't know how he was going to die, but he knew his death would glorify God. Joseph didn't know how he would end up in the palace, but he knew that God had a plan to prosper him and not to harm him. A sip of what is ahead of you is all you need to keep going, to keep believing, to keep striving for everything God has for you.

Scripture

Soon Joseph had another dream, and again he told his brothers about it. "Listen, I have had another dream," he said. "The sun, moon, and eleven stars bowed low before me!"

Genesis 37:9 NLT

Prayer

In order to reach my final destination, I must endure the trials and tribulations. You may give me a sip of where I am headed, but that is only to encourage me to keep on pushing. I may become thirsty, but I won't pass out. I may want to try something else, but I will stay focused on the things in which You have in store for me. In Jesus name, amen.

Day 85

Love Past the Flaws

Just as Jesus loves us past our flaws, so shall we love others past theirs. Maybe your friends or family members have betrayed you or have done things that hurt you, but you must be the bigger person and love them. Maybe your best friend left you alone in a moment you needed them most. As easy as it may be to slander their name, be the bigger person and love them. When you were manipulative, a liar, and a cheater, God still loved you. When you were addicted to drugs and struggled with alcohol, God still loved you. While others were disgusted with you because of your imperfections, God loved you. Just as God continues to show us unconditional love, we should continue to show others unconditional love. You may be able to love someone close to you while you may have to love someone else from a distance. Regardless of what they did or what they said about you, continue to love them. In the moments where it's easy to hate, choose to love.

Scripture

Most important of all, continue to show deep love for each other, for love covers a multitude of sins.

1 Peter 4:8 NLT

Prayer

Just as You love me for who I am, I shall love others for who they are. Nobody is perfect. I have no right to judge others because of their mistakes, but You have commanded me to love others regardless of what they've done. Give me the strength to love more than I ever have before. In Jesus name, amen.

Day 86

Don't Stop at the Victory

The reason why billions of people never step foot into their destiny is because they stopped working after one victory. They looked at that victory as a huge accomplishment, which I am sure it was, but it wasn't the place where God wanted them to rest. When Joshua defeated one army, God told him to go fight another. After he would defeat another army, God would tell him to go after another. God had already declared Joshua victorious before every battle. Joshua could've laid down, had a couple of drinks, go party after his one victory, but he knew there was more work that had to be done in order to reach his destiny. Think about a student who just aced their first exam. A lazy student, a student with no drive or no purpose will say, "I don't need to put forth any effort on any more exams." That same student will most likely fail because they thought the success of one exam would be enough to pass the class. If a student wants an A out of a class, they must strive to ace every single exam. After they ace one exam, either that same night or the next day they should start preparing for the next exam. When you are focused on selling your most recent book, you should be developing ideas for your next book. When you reach your goal in the gym, set another goal. Don't stop at the victory! Victories are a small part of your destiny. If you won today, I want you to win tomorrow. Don't stop at the victory!

Scripture

When Joshua was an old man, the Lord said to him, "You are growing old, and much land remains to be conquered.

Joshua 13:1 NLT

Prayer

I will not rest after a victory. I will not slumber after I have defeated a giant. I will keep on fighting the good fight of faith! Thank you Lord for giving me the strength to keep on running! In Jesus name, amen.

Day 87

Limits

When you think of limits, you think about how far you can go until it seems impossible to go any further. For athletes, this may mean how much they can stress their body before their muscles give out forcing them to sit down. Students may put a limit on how much time they can spend with their friends before they must go back and prepare for their next exam. Parents put limits on how late their son or daughter can be out with their friends or how many sweets they can eat in one day. States put speed limits on roads to ensure the safety of every driver and pedestrian. While limits are put in place to keep one safe, limits can also prevent one from achieving greatness. I'm not talking about a speed limit or the amount of alcohol you can consume before getting drunk. I'm talking about a limited mentality. What have you told yourself that is impossible? What have you not accomplished because of your fear of failure? We tend to put limits on ourselves in areas where God has given us the strength to overcome. Stop thinking yourself limited and start thinking yourself blessed! If you have a limited mentality, you'll put a limit on everything you do. If you have a blessed mentality, you'll live a blessed life.

Scripture

Jesus looked at them intently and said, "Humanly speaking, it is impossible. But with God everything is possible."

Matthew 19:26 NLT

Prayer

While my credit card may have a limit, You have no limit. I serve a limitless God. Man may tell me that I will never get to where I am trying to go, but You always make a way. You always come through! With God, all things are possible! You will answer all of my prayers! You will bring to fruition everything I have written down! You have no limits, God! In Jesus name, amen.

Day 88

Focus on You

You don't owe anybody an apology for wanting to be great. You don't owe anybody an explanation for not wanting to fit in with the crowd. Stop wasting time worrying about what others think. While they're talking about you, you should be working on yourself! The amount of time that is spent talking about somebody else or watching somebody make their dreams come true is ridiculous! While your friends waste time on Facebook arguing with people who they will most likely never meet, you could be making that idea of yours come to life. While people are making excuses about their weight or their lack of fitness, you can be in the gym or at home training. Think about how much further ahead you can get in life if you just focus on you. Think about how much peace you'll be at when you stop worrying about man judging you. God created you to be you! He didn't create you to be like your mom, your dad, your brother, your sister, or your friends. He created you to be you, and the only way you can achieve everything He has planned for you is if you focus on God and yourself!

Scripture

Commit your actions to the Lord, and your plans will succeed.

Proverbs 16:3 NLT

Prayer

Everything I do will be committed to You. Everything I plan for will be according to Your purpose for my life. I will not focus on what others are doing or what they have to say about me. I am focused on You and who You created me to be. As long as I am focused on You and Your will for my life, I know that You will take me to places that I never imagined. In Jesus name, amen.

Day 89

Your Vision

Stop getting mad at people who don't understand your vision. Stop becoming frustrated with people who don't believe in your vision. Don't quit when others are unable to see your vision. It's your vision! If it were meant for your friends to see or for your parents to understand, God would have given them the vision, but He didn't! He gave it to you! I understand it may be difficult when nobody else can see where you want to go. I understand what it's like to talk about a place that others have yet to imagine, but that's called faith! Do you have faith that God will make your vision a reality? Do you believe that you can achieve everything you see in your mind? Stop worrying about the haters and the doubters! They are blind! Don't listen to the fearful! They can't see themselves going where God is taking you! It's your vision so run after it!

Scripture

"Write the vision and make it plain on tablets, That he may run who reads it."

Habakkuk 2:2 NKJV

Prayer

Expand my vision, Lord. Make my vision clear. I now understand that the vision You have given me was meant for me to see and not others. If it were meant for someone else to see, You would've given them the vision. I know that the vision You have given me shall come to pass. In Jesus name, amen.

Day 90

Your Exit

God gives us plenty of opportunities to exit sin. He gives us so many chances to get our lives together, but there are still too many people who choose to play with sin. If you choose to swim with the devil, he will plunge you under water with no intention of ever giving you a chance to breathe again. If you choose to ride with the enemy, you will find yourself in an accident that you may not ever recover from. If you choose to fly with the enemy, he will encourage you to jump without a parachute. Jesus knew that the enemy had traps in place. That's why He died for you and me. He died for us so that we wouldn't be trapped in the eternal pit of fire. Jesus is your exit. He is your exit from the substance abuse. He is your exit from the sexual immorality. He is your exit from the gang. Choose to exit while you can. If you're reading this today, you have an opportunity to exit your life of sin. Give your life to God before it's too late. You can't exit hell! There's no grace, no forgiveness, no peace, and no second chances in hell. This is the only time you get a second chance. While you're breathing, choose to give your life over to God. He promised us that there is a place that He has prepared for you and I that is perfect. Exit your life of sin while you can!

Scripture

But if we confess our sins to him, he is faithful and just to forgive us our sins and to cleanse us from all wickedness.

1 John 1:9 NLT

Prayer

God, forgive me for every lie I have ever told. Forgive me for every sexual relationship I have had outside of marriage. Forgive me for any evil things I may have spoken. Today, I give my life to You. Cleanse me of my sins so that I may enjoy an eternal life with You. In Jesus name, amen.

Day 91

You Won't Break

There are many trials in life that will make you feel as if you're about to break. When your marriage is twisted and upside down, you'll be tempted to be break. When you can't afford to pay the rent or mortgage and you receive an eviction notice, you'll be tempted to break. When your car breaks down in the middle of the road after you've been laid off from your job, you'll be tempted to be break. When the man you thought you were going to marry chooses another woman to be his wife, you'll be tempted to break. I want to remind you today that no man, no woman, or no job can break you. You were built to withstand that trial. You were built to withstand that marriage. You were built to stand tall in the midst of the fire. You were built to walk on water. You were built to get up after the enemy knocked you down. When the enemy has you surrounded, don't bow down. God is with you in the midst of your battles. You were built to stand, not to break!

Scripture

"For I know the plans I have for you," says the Lord. "They are plans for good and not for disaster, to give you a future and a hope."

Jeremiah 29:11 NLT

Prayer

I will not break. I will not stumble. The plans You have for me shall prosper me. No matter what the enemy may throw my way, it will not break me. You built me to stand firm in my faith and to not break to the ways of this world. In Jesus name, amen.

Day 92

God's Promises

After Joshua and the Israelites defeated all of their enemies, God swore that He would give the Israelites land and that's exactly what He did. Every single tribe was given territory just as God had promised. Have you ever asked God to expand your territory? Have you ever questioned if His promises would come to pass? There's no reason to question God. If He told you that you will become wealthy or you will become a mother, trust that everything He has said will come to fruition. There is no reason to implement your own plan because it most likely doesn't align with God's. Before the Israelites could dwell in the land that God had promised them, they had to endure many hard-fought battles. Before you can dwell in the promises of God, you must continue to fight the good fight of faith. There will be moments where it will be difficult. There will be times where you may have to make sacrifices. It doesn't matter what you go through or what the devil throws at you, God's promises will be fulfilled. He has never broken any of His promises and He won't ever break any of His promises.

Scripture

No, I will not break my covenant; I will not take back a single word I said.

Psalms 89:34 NLT

Prayer

Lord, I know that Your word shall forever stand. Your promises never become lost. Your covenant shall always remain intact. In Jesus name, amen.

Day 93

Stay on Track

Right before Joshua died, he instructed the Israelites to follow everything Moses wrote. He told them to not go right nor left. In life, there are many times when we are tempted to get off track. Your friends may invite you to the club on a Saturday night when you should be studying for your exam on Monday. Your guys may ask you to get online and play Call of Duty with them when you should be writing that new book of yours. Maybe your wife wants to binge watch a Netflix series when God wants you to indulge His word. It's easy to get off track when you're tired, sore, or in a little bit of pain, but think about everything else that may fall off because you fell off. There are marriages that fall apart because one person got off track. There are households destroyed because one person got off track. I understand the land outside of the track is great, but that narrow road is the only path that will lead you to your destiny. That narrow road is the only path that will get you to heaven. That narrow road is the only path that will lead you to God. It appears long and at times it may seem lonely, but God is always with you. It may be quiet, but God is speaking to you. As long as you stay on God's track, you will reach your destination where there are many rewards that await you.

Scripture

You will show me the path of life; In Your presence is fullness of joy; At Your right hand are pleasures forevermore.

Psalms 16:11 NKJV

Prayer

I will stay on the path of life. While that path may be narrow, it is worth it. While the world may make it seem as if partying, getting drunk, and having sex outside of marriage is fun, that path only leads to death. Although your path may be difficult to follow at times and requires a lot of faith, I know in the end I will make You proud. In Jesus name, amen.

Day 94

I've Been Saved for...

It doesn't matter. Jesus saved us all over two thousand years ago. He paid the same price for all of us so that we have a chance to live in His kingdom for an eternity. Whether you've known Christ for a year or 30 years, God loves you. Just because you got baptized and were filled with the Holy Spirit when you were 15 doesn't mean you won't make a mistake when you're 30. As the body of Christ, we need to accept those who are lost with open arms. Stop looking down on the stranger that just entered your church. They may be a stranger to you, but they are no stranger to God. Stop making excuses for your sin. David was anointed when He was a boy, but that didn't stop him from confessing his sins to God. God didn't recognize David for the number of years he had been anointed. He recognized David as a man after His own heart. Are you still seeking to have a heart like God's, or have you become arrogant in the church? From this day forward, start helping those who are lost instead of talking down on them. Instead of giving someone you don't know a disgusting look, start smiling and take the initiative to greet them. You shouldn't care about people knowing how long you have been saved. You should want them to realize that you have a heart for God.

Scripture

But God removed Saul and replaced him with David, a man about whom God said, 'I have found David son of Jesse, a man after my own heart. He will do everything I want him to do.'

Acts 13:22 NLT

Prayer

Lord, continue to renew my heart. Renew my mind. It doesn't matter how long I've been saved and going to church---I'll always need you. Just like anyone else, I am prone to making mistakes. The only reason I am alive today is because of Your everlasting grace. In Jesus name, amen.

Day 95

Move

When you want to move forward, you must be willing to walk forward. If you want to go to another level, you must think on another level. If you want to be successful in the future, you must make sacrifices today. You cannot and will not be successful by putting no action behind your faith. God moves when you move. When you invest time into what you desire to do, He will reward you. When you run, God will give you the endurance to go further. You won't get anywhere by sitting on the couch watching Netflix every day you have off. Your body won't change if you don't exercise. If you want to be in a different place tomorrow than you are today, you have to move. You will improve as you move.

Scripture

The Lord says, "I will guide you along the best pathway for your life. I will advise you and watch over you."

Psalms 32:8 NLT

Prayer

I will no longer be afraid of taking another step. I will not doubt Your leadership. I have faith that You will not allow me to stumble. While I may not be able to see what is ahead of me, I know that You are always watching over me. In Jesus name, amen.

Day 96

Self-Discipline

Great success requires a greater amount of self-discipline. Leaders aren't influenced by the crowd, but the crowd is influenced by the leader. Are you a leader? When your friends ask you to come out and have a drink with them, do you have the courage to say no or do you fall in line at the bar taking one shot after another? When everybody else is spending their money on clothes, on video games, and on shoes, are you investing in your future or will you choose to suffer later because of a popular shoe that came out today? When your peers want to go out for ice cream, but you have a physical goal that you want to meet by the end of the month, will you sacrifice that goal to satisfy your friends? You must have self-discipline. As you climb the ladder, it will be tempting to come back down, but you must have the heart to keep climbing. When everyone is telling you to go this or to go that way, choose God's way. If you have self-discipline today, you will win tomorrow.

Scripture

You didn't choose me. I chose you. I appointed you to go and produce lasting fruit, so that the Father will give you whatever you ask for, using my name.

Hebrews 12:11 NLT

Prayer

Lord, anoint my no. When my friends invite me to get drunk with them, give me the strength to say no. When the woman I have been working with for 10 years begins to flirt with me, give me the strength to walk away. While many temptations may come, I now have the strength to say no. I will remain focused on You. I will not fall into the devil's hands. In Jesus name, amen.

Day 97

Chosen

You were chosen to be where you are today for a reason. Whether you know what you were chosen for or not, you have a purpose. Maybe you weren't chosen to be a part of the basketball team or to be prom queen, but that doesn't mean you weren't chosen to do or be anything else. If God chose you it's because you proved that He could trust you. He chose you to be the CEO of that company because of your sacrifices. He chose you to teach that student because of the impact you would have in their life. He chose you to be homeless for a season because He knew that would be your testimony next season. Too many people today have become depressed because they feel like they will never be chosen! What many fail to realize is that they have already been chosen. Don't quit, don't become depressed, don't think of yourself worthless because I promise, you have a purpose! If nobody else has, I want to remind you that you're chosen! Now go out there and do what God has called you to do.

Scripture

You didn't choose me. I chose you. I appointed you to go and produce lasting fruit, so that the Father will give you whatever you ask for, using my name.

John 15:16 NLT

Prayer

God, thank you for choosing me. Thank You for choosing to love me and to die for me. Thank You for choosing me to be the husband to my wife or the wife to my husband. Thank You for choosing me to be the father or the mother of my children. Thank You for choosing me to be in the position I am today. You chose me before I was in my mother's womb. Thank You, Lord. In Jesus name, amen.

Day 98

Fly High

Many people want to fly, but few are willing to jump. Many people want to jump, but they're also afraid of heights. In order for an eagle to fly it has to jump from its nest. The eagle may be born with wings, but it won't be able to soar in the sky if it won't overcome its fear to jump. The eagle doesn't know it has the ability to fly until it jumps from its mother's nest. Did you know you can fly also? Did you know God has given you wings that will give you the ability to fly higher than all your enemies? If you answered no, it's because you have yet to jump. You're afraid that if you jump you will fail, and everybody will laugh at you. You're afraid to jump because of the rocks that lie below. Don't let those rocks stop you from flying. You have something the rocks don't and that is wings. When you jump, you may be falling while flapping or flapping while falling, but before you know it you will soon be flying. After you begin to fly, you'll begin to soar. God wants you to fly high! He wants to bring you to places that your enemies can't even imagine. If you want to fly high tomorrow, you must be willing to jump today!

Scripture

But those who trust in the Lord will find new strength. They will soar high on wings like eagles. They will run and not grow weary. They will walk and not faint.

Isaiah 40:31 NLT

Prayer

While others think about running with the lions, I know that You have given me the ability to fly high with the eagles. I will be in an atmosphere full of life. I will not have a sky is the limit mentality. I will fly above the clouds. I will use the wings You have given me to soar. In Jesus name, amen.

Day 99

Almost

While we live in a time where people praise someone for almost reaching their destination, almost should never be the goal. You don't want to almost reach your destiny; you want to be in your destiny. You don't want to almost finish reading this devotional; you want to complete it and apply it. You don't want to almost make it into heaven, you want to live in heaven! Don't give up when you've reached almost. When you're almost there, keep going. When you're close to reaching the finish line, keep running. When you're close to the peak of the mountain, keep climbing. Don't settle for almost. Strive to achieve the most! Strive to be the greatest person God created you to be. I don't want you to almost make it. I want you to make it!

Scripture

"But as for you, be strong and courageous, for your work will be rewarded."

2 Chronicles 15:7 NLT

Prayer

I almost didn't wake up today, but You knew that I still have a purpose here on Earth. I almost didn't go after my dreams, but I didn't want to die without fulfilling what You have called me to do. I don't serve an almost God. You follow through with Your words. You stay true to Your promises. In Jesus name, amen.

Day 100

Draw the Line

This is the day where you draw the line. Satan has crossed the boundaries too much! You've allowed him to come in between you and your spouse. You've allowed him to play with your mind. You've allowed him to tear down your house. You've allowed him to mess with your kids. Enough is enough! You must draw the line and let the devil know that he can no longer play with your mind. He can no longer mess with your kids. He can no longer come into your house. He can longer mess with you and your spouse! Draw the line, put on the armor, and let the enemy know that if he even thinks about crossing that line, there will be repercussions! You will no longer tolerate his presence! If you haven't already, draw the line! Satan will bother you no more!

Scripture

Speak these things, exhort, and rebuke with all authority. Let no one despise you.

Titus 2:15 NKJV

Prayer

As I complete this devotional, I am choosing to draw the line. The enemy cannot and will not come into my mind. He will not come into my house. He will not bother my children. He will not steal my joy, destroy my peace, or kill my mind. I am drawing the line! I am protected! God's hand is on my life! I rebuke every single evil spirit that will ever try to attack me. In Jesus name, amen.

Chains have been BROKEN!

Do you feel like you can breathe? Do you feel free? There were areas of your mind that were once dead that are now alive! There were areas of your heart that were holding onto anger and unforgiveness that are now healthy and whole because you decided to love and forgive! Chains have been broken which now gives you the ability to go further than you could have ever imagined! Now that you have broken out of the place where the devil was trying to hold you hostage, I want you to apply every principle you have learned from this 100-day devotional! I want you to remain free! Pass *I'm Breaking Out* onto someone you know who may be trapped. Start a book club with your family or a group of friends. Be courageous and help others who may feel like being free again is impossible. God bless you!

www.ingramcontent.com/pod-product-compliance
Lightning Source LLC
Chambersburg PA
CBHW071343080526
44587CB00017B/2938